THE
AVE
PRAYER BOOK
FOR
CATHOLIC
MOTHERS

"With so many contributors from different life perspectives, the beautiful diversity of Catholic motherhood really shines through the pages of this book. Each contributor shares from her heart about a personal experience of prayer and the end result is both a joyful celebration of the faith we all share in common and an inspiring look at the beautiful ways that Catholic moms are different."

Danielle Bean
Brand manager of CatholicMom.com

"*The Ave Prayer Book for Catholic Mothers* is an excellent resource for ordinary moms who want to tap into the graces of an extraordinary God. Drawing from scripture and the powerful litanies of the Church, it will help you turn useless worry into powerful prayer. Keep a copy in your purse and another by your bed. You'll find it to be just what you need!"

Lisa Brenninkmeyer
Founder and chief purpose officer of Walking with Purpose

"From cultivating more intimacy in married life, to childbirth, raising your crew, blessing your children as they leave home, and even caring for elderly parents, this prayer book has you covered! What a gift for those navigating every stage of motherhood!"

Sarah Swafford
Catholic speaker and author of *Emotional Virtue*

"*The Ave Prayer Book for Catholic Mothers* is a real treasure; a great gathering of prayers for all seasons of the heart and of wisdom gleaned from the experience of many wonderful women of faith. I'll be gifting copies of this book to many mothers and I'll get a copy for myself (and some men I know) as well!"

Rev. James H. Phalan, C.S.C.
National Director of Family Rosary

THE
AVE
PRAYER BOOK
FOR
CATHOLIC
MOTHERS

EDITED BY HEIDI HESS SAXTON

AVE MARIA PRESS AVE Notre Dame, Indiana

© 2021 by Ave Maria Press, Inc.

All rights reserved. No part of this book may be used or reproduced in any manner whatsoever, except in the case of reprints in the context of reviews, without written permission from Ave Maria Press®, Inc., P.O. Box 428, Notre Dame, IN 46556, 1-800-282-1865.

Founded in 1865, Ave Maria Press is a ministry of the United States Province of Holy Cross.

www.avemariapress.com

Hardcover: ISBN-13 978-1-64680-109-1

E-book: ISBN-13 978-1-64680-110-7

Cover and interior images © GettyImages.com.

Cover and text design by Katherine Robinson.

Printed and bound in Canada.

Library of Congress Cataloging-in-Publication Data
Names: Saxton, Heidi Hess, editor.
Title: The Ave prayer book for Catholic mothers / edited by Heidi Hess Saxton.
Description: Notre Dame, Indiana : Ave Maria Press, [2021] | Includes bibliographical references and index. | Summary: "In this book, dozens of Catholic mothers of every age and background, with children at every stage of life, share their favorite prayers and prayer stories"-- Provided by publisher.
Identifiers: LCCN 2021019028 | ISBN 9781646801091 (hardcover) | ISBN 9781646801107 (ebook)
Subjects: LCSH: Mothers--Prayers and devotions. | Catholic women--Prayers and devotions. | Children--Prayers and devotions.
Classification: LCC BX2353 .A94 2021 | DDC 242/.643--dc23
LC record available at https://lccn.loc.gov/2021019028

Contents

Part VII: Prayers for Peace in Times of Grief and Loss—"Love Is Strong as Death" (Song of Solomon 8:6)

A Note from the Publisher

Welcome to *The Ave Prayer Book for Catholic Mothers*, a spiritual lifeline you can call upon when you talk with God. Written by more than eighty contributors at various stages of motherhood, this treasury will connect you with other women who understand your hopes, dreams, frustrations, heartaches, and joys. These extraordinary women—including Lisa M. Hendey, Jenna Guizar, Emily Wilson Hussem, Haley Stewart, Kelly Wahlquist, and Leticia Ochoa Adams—share favorite prayers, litanies, songs, and reflections that you can offer to the Lord for almost every intention.

This beautifully designed collection includes "A Kitchen Sink Offering," "The Nine Annoying Things Novena," "The Litany of Weakness," "A Marian Lullaby," "When Choices Have Consequences," "The Rosary for Warriors," and "Will Anything Be Okay Again?" Traditional Catholic prayers—the Mysteries of the Rosary, the Memorare, and the Jesus Prayer, for example—are included as well, and many of these are personal favorites of those of us here at Ave.

My most vivid memories of my paternal grandmother, Grandma Welde, are visiting with her and praying with her. She prayed the Rosary daily and had an old blue cloth prayer book on her nightstand that she read from each evening. My hope is that this volume finds a permanent home on your nightstand and becomes a regular part of your prayer life.

Books on prayer and spirituality, particularly for women, are an important part of what we do at Ave Maria Press. As a ministry of the Congregation of Holy Cross, United States Province of Priests and Brothers, our mission is to be educators in the faith; to make God known, loved, and served; and to spread the Gospel through our publications. I am proud to add *The Ave Prayer Book for Catholic Mothers* to our award-winning family of resources.

I hope this book will be a treasured keepsake and your go-to resource for the perfect words to lift up in prayer no matter what the need is in your life.

May God bless you abundantly with his great love.

Karey Circosta

Karey Circosta
CEO and Publisher, Ave Maria Press

THE AVE PRAYER BOOK FOR CATHOLIC MOTHERS

FOREWORD

Growing up with a mother who prayed had a great impact on me as a child. And having a mother who *still* prays has a great impact on my life now as a mother.

My mother is a convert to Catholicism. I am her second child, and she converted when she was pregnant with me (I have yet to meet anyone else whose mother received the Sacraments of Initiation while they were in her womb!). She attended daily Mass as often as possible, and even as tiny children we accompanied her on each of those mornings. When I was in elementary school, I knew each day that my mom would be at Mass on campus at our Catholic school. I remember when, in eighth grade, I was chosen by my class to be the May Queen and I wanted to tell my mom . . . I looked at the clock and knew that she would be in the church as Mass was ending. I found her and told her the news. I loved knowing where she would be—I loved knowing she would be in our church, talking with the Lord. My mother's deep devotion to Jesus, especially in daily Mass, changed my life and has inspired me to do the same, as much as I can, with my own children.

The simple fact is that, as mothers, not all of us can attend Mass every day; our other responsibilities may prevent us fitting it into our weekday schedule. And yet, it was not only my mom's daily devotion to the Eucharist that transformed my life—it was her dedication to being a mother who prayed, which is what this book is about. This book is about helping you to be a mother who prays. It is about striving to become a mother who has prayer and a connection with the Lord at the center of everything you do. The Lord does not ask us to be perfect in our mothering—but he asks us to root it in him.

My friend Fr. Louis once described prayer as "a response to infinite love." I pray this book can be a guide in helping you respond to the infinite, passionate love God has for you. May it offer you many moments, in the midst of the many tasks to be accomplished, to be

with the Lord, to speak to him, and to rededicate your mothering to him again and again. May the traditional prayers held here give you words to speak to God on the days when you feel you cannot think of one more thing, even words in prayer. May the testimonies fill you with consolation in knowing you are not alone on this road with its abundant joys and difficulties. And may every page of this book lead you closer to our generous and kind Lord, who chose you for this holy responsibility, the vocation of trying to raise your children to be saints.

Emily Wilson Hussem

Introduction

I am fascinated by prayer stories—testimonies of faith and perseverance from women who do their best every day to listen for God's voice and to do what he asks of them. I grew up in a Christian household and was taught to believe in a God who answers prayers, who is always ready to meet an urgent need or work a small miracle in a dire situation. To be honest, I've had more than my fair share of small miracles.

What took me a lot longer to embrace—not until I became Catholic in my early thirties, in fact—was that God doesn't always "grease the wheels" for us. Great mercy can come out of great suffering, and there is a dark side to expecting God to provide not only our daily bread but the margaritas and cake as well. I was eighteen when my own faith was tested on this score, when an accident totaled the family car and very nearly killed me. Once I was able to walk again, I enrolled in a missionary training school in Minnesota, spent a year interning in Senegal, West Africa, and eventually moved to California. There (long story short) I wound up becoming Catholic at a particularly dark time of my life in 1994, when I was desperate to find a place where it didn't feel like my prayers were bouncing off the ceiling.

I had been sneaking into Catholic Masses for about six months when I made an appointment with Dawn, the director of religious education at a nearby parish, who shuddered when I told her I'd been receiving the Eucharist. She told me to stop, which I did. Then she assigned me a sponsor, who quit within three weeks because I asked too many questions. Finally, Dawn took me under her wing. And before I knew it, I was standing beneath the palm trees at Holy Family Catholic Parish in South Pasadena, waiting to light my taper at the Easter Vigil. And then, an hour later, I received Jesus in the Eucharist for the first time as a Catholic.

As it turns out, my Catholic education was just beginning. I had yet to discover novenas or litanies. I avoided the Rosary like the plague because "why pray to Mary when I can go right to God?" It wasn't until

I married Craig and we began to foster, and later adopted, our two children that I figured out the answer to that question. Because *that*, my friend, is where I really learned to pray. There is nothing quite like the isolated helplessness and unmitigated failure that are part and parcel of the vocation of motherhood to kick your prayer life into overdrive. I knew beyond a shadow of a doubt that I needed help, and that my type-A personality was going to kill us all if God didn't show a little mercy and make me into a calmer, gentler, kinder version of myself.

Almost twenty years later, I'm still waiting for that miracle. And that is *my* prayer story, summed up in this beautiful hymn by one of my spiritual heroes, Amy Carmichael (to the tune of "Faith of Our Fathers"):

Make Me Thy Fuel

From prayer that asks that I may be
Sheltered from winds that beat on Thee,
From fainting when I should aspire
From faltering when I should climb higher!
From silken self, O Captain free
Thy soldier who would follow Thee.

From subtle love of softening things
From easy choices, weakenings.
Not thus are spirits fortified
Not this way went Thy Crucified
From all that dims Thy Calvary
O Lamb of God, deliver me!

Give me the love that leads the way
The courage nothing can dismay
The hope no disappointments tire
The passion that will burn like fire
Let me not sink to be a clod.
Make me thy fuel, O Flame of God![1]

Why Use a Prayer Book?

Prayer is to the Christian life, and particularly to the vocation of motherhood, what oxygen is to fire: You may be able to get along without it for short periods of time, but deprived for too long, you'll burn out. Even when a leisurely holy hour seems like too much to ask, and you are reduced to nodding at the tabernacle on Sunday mornings while corralling a pewful of rambunctious toddlers, take heart: You have reinforcements, even if you can't see them. So when you are feeling particularly frazzled, take a page from this book and let the words soothe your soul.

The beauty of "rote" (written) prayers is that they enrich the offerings we send heavenward, combining our thoughts with the wisdom of holy men and women through the ages as well as the prayers of our brothers and sisters around the world. Yes, God loves to hear our voices, and stands ready to converse with us every time we quiet our hearts and invite him to speak to us. And speak he does: sometimes in that still, small voice he used with Elijah in the wilderness (1 Kgs 19:12), sometimes through the words of scripture . . . and sometimes through the prayers of our spiritual brothers and sisters who understand our joys and struggles and can articulate them even better.

How to Use This Book

This book is a compilation of the favorite prayers and prayer stories of some amazing Catholic moms, from every walk of life and with children at every stage of life. As you flip through the pages, you will discover that each prayer is enhanced with a reflection or story from another Catholic mother that will inspire you or help the prayer to come to life in your own heart. In some cases the prayers have been borrowed from a great Catholic pray-er (such as one of the saints); other times, these are original prayers these moms have written themselves for particular needs or occasions.

A special section of this book is dedicated to the prayers of the traditional Rosary, as well as other Rosary forms and some chaplets (devotions adapted to rosary beads). There is also a section of litanies (a series of petitions that are led by one person with a response from the rest of the group), and there are numerous prayers for particular seasons of life or situations.

Think of this prayer book as a kind of spiritual gym where you can go for a daily workout. Does your marriage need a little pick-me-up? Turn to that section. Are you feeling the growing pains of motherhood? There's a section for those trials. Do you just want to spend five minutes with Jesus in the tabernacle, or offer a meaningful prayer after receiving the Eucharist? Turn to the first section to find the prayer you need.

The benefits of this type of spiritual exercise correspond to a great degree to the benefits of physical exercise: health, fitness, strength, endurance. We go before God each day to build up the spiritual stamina we need to make it through the sprints of life—those emergencies when we need our spiritual muscles to be in top form—as well as the marathons, when we need to endure a difficult situation over the long term, trusting God to strengthen and protect us as we go. If you are looking for a prayer to address a particular situation or need, or by a particular author, turn to the indexes at the back of this book.

In closing, I'd like to thank each of the women who gave of their time and energy to bring this project to life. Their heartfelt testimonies are such a gift to me—and I know they will be to you, too. You can find out more about each of them in the "Contributors" section at the back of the book.

Would you like to share your prayer story? Drop me a note at heidi.hess.saxton@gmail.com or find me online at *Life on the Road Less Traveled*. I look forward to hearing from you.

God bless you!

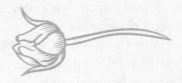

Part I

Prayers for Encountering God

~~~~~

"Worship the Lord with gladness."
Psalm 100:2 (NRSV)

Whether we make our morning offering in a quiet corner of our home, while on our morning run, or in the solitude of a prayer chapel, our Lord welcomes us with open arms. He knows what is on our hearts, yet for our sake he invites us to share everything that is there so that he can fortify us for the day ahead.

The prayers in this section have been selected to help you find the words to deepen that sense of encounter. No matter what it is you need—a fresh slate, inner peace, courage to do the hard thing, or a way to express your gratitude for our Lord's presence in your life—you will find the words here to "prime the pump" so you can continue the conversation in your own words, either in spoken prayer or in a prayer journal.

Don't be afraid! St. Paul reminds us, "Have no anxiety about anything, but in everything by prayer and supplication with thanksgiving let your requests be made known to God. And the peace of God, which passes all understanding, will keep your hearts and your minds in Christ Jesus" (Phil 4:6–7).

LORD, I BELIEVE IN YOU

Katie Prejean McGrady

While I was a sophomore in college, I had the opportunity to study in Rome for a semester. At nineteen I found myself roaming the streets of the Eternal City—eating my weight in gelato, visiting museums, and popping in and out of churches with countless saints' relics and gorgeous art. Each time I walked into one of these churches, I'd find myself wondering what I should do (besides take pictures). It's not like I had the time to pray a full Rosary in each church (nor did I have the desire to), but it didn't feel like a quick Our Father was enough to pray in front of the tabernacle inside these old, profoundly beautiful houses of worship. So I asked the campus chaplain to recommend a prayer, and he handed me a copy of "The Universal Prayer" by Pope Clement XI (1649–1721).

I was captivated by the lyrical flow of the words, the depth of their meaning, and just how wide-ranging the petitions were. It quickly became my go-to "what to say when I'm in front of Jesus" prayer. It truly is universal, a "tell him everything without having to figure out something to say" sort of prayer. It covers the desire to be obedient and the need to remain focused on God's will above all else. It expresses the hope that we will adore the Lord well. It gives voice to the understanding that we are made for heaven and should long for it above all else. Truthfully, what more could we say when sitting in front of the tabernacle, in Jesus' presence, pouring out our heart?

With kids underfoot, a home to care for, work to be done, and life to be lived, I often find myself frazzled or at a loss for words when I have time before the Eucharist. Or, I have so much to say that I don't feel that I have enough time to say it all! "The Universal Prayer" of Pope Clement XI fills in all the gaps. It captures most of what's on my mind, reminds me of the power and glory of the Lord in the Eucharist, and helps me to rest in his presence.

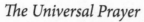

The Universal Prayer

Lord, I believe in you: increase my faith.
I trust in you: strengthen my trust.
I love you: let me love you more and more.
I am sorry for my sins: deepen my sorrow.
I worship you as my first beginning,
I long for you as my last end,
I praise you as my constant helper,
And call on you as my loving protector.

Guide me by your wisdom,
Correct me with your justice,
Comfort me with your mercy,
Protect me with your power.

I offer you, Lord, my thoughts: to be fixed on you;
My words: to have you for their theme;
My actions: to reflect my love for you;
My sufferings: to be endured for your greater glory.

I want to do what you ask of me:
In the way you ask,
For as long as you ask,
Because you ask it.

Lord, enlighten my understanding,
Strengthen my will,
Purify my heart,
And make me holy.

Help me to repent of my past sins
And to resist temptation in the future.
Help me to rise above my human weaknesses
And to grow stronger as a Christian.

Let me love you, my Lord and my God,
And see myself as I really am:
A pilgrim in this world,
A Christian called to respect and love
All whose lives I touch,
Those under my authority,
My friends and my enemies.

Help me to conquer anger with gentleness,
Greed by generosity,
Apathy by fervor.
Help me to forget myself
And reach out toward others.

Make me prudent in planning,
Courageous in taking risks.
Make me patient in suffering, unassuming in prosperity.

Keep me, Lord, attentive at prayer,
Temperate in food and drink,
Diligent in my work,
Firm in my good intentions.

Let my conscience be clear,
My conduct without fault,
My speech blameless,
My life well-ordered.
Put me on guard against my human weaknesses.
Let me cherish your love for me,
Keep your law,
And come at last to your salvation.

Teach me to realize that this world is passing,
That my true future is the happiness of heaven,
That life on earth is short,
And the life to come eternal.

Help me to prepare for death
With a proper fear of judgment,
But a greater trust in your goodness.
Lead me safely through death
To the endless joy of heaven.
Grant this through Christ our Lord. Amen.[2]

When You Don't Feel like Praying

Daria Sockey

My daily prayer routine is centered on the Liturgy of the Hours—a repeating cycle of psalms, scriptures, readings from the saints, and other prayers that follow the liturgical seasons. This is all contained in a prayer book known as the Breviary, which I crack open every morning, afternoon, evening, and night for roughly ten minutes at a time. I've learned that maintaining the habit of prayer means *just doing it* each day, whether or not I feel like it, rather than waiting for the perfect prayerful mood to strike.

But what about those times when you're feeling so distracted or stressed that prayer threatens to become just one more item to check off an endless to-do list? Nothing but a recitation to be gotten over with before starting a new chore?

A few years ago, while doing the Office of Readings, I came across a passage from St. Anselm's *Proslogion*. (It appears every year on Friday of the first week of Advent.) I was so struck by it that I copied it on an index card and keep it tucked in my Breviary. Any time that I approach my daily prayer with a head full of racing thoughts, I take a few deep breaths and read this meditation, which ends with a short but beautiful prayer that gets my mind on the right track. As I read St. Anselm's "Prelude to Prayer," I visualize myself doing the actions it describes. It never fails to take me away from my worries and into a place of calm—a place where I am truly ready to seek the Lord's face.

St. Anselm's Prelude to Prayer

Insignificant man, escape from your everyday business for a short while, hide for a moment from your restless thoughts. Break off from your cares and troubles and be less concerned about your tasks and labors. Make a little time for God and rest a while in him. Enter into your mind's inner chamber. Shut out everything but God and whatever helps you to seek him; and when you have shut the door, look for him. Speak now to God and say with your whole heart: "I seek your Face; your Face, Lord, I desire."[3]

When You Really Need Mercy
Justina Kopp

The Jesus Prayer came into my life in a moment when I desperately needed mercy. After college, I was reeling from a painful relationship and breakup, and even though I was working as a campus minister, my faith was feeling strained. My heart and mind deeply needed renewal and healing.

After a particularly grueling Lent, I managed to find a last-minute Confession time on Holy Saturday morning. Holy Saturday has always been my favorite day of the liturgical year, but I was feeling disconnected. I made my way over to the cathedral and joined the surprisingly long line for Confession, mentally gathering up my unsurprisingly long list of sins.

Finally, it was my turn. When it was time for the Act of Contrition, the priest requested that I use the Jesus Prayer, due to the number of people waiting. I hadn't done this before, but I found it was concise and to the point: I just asked Christ to have mercy on me, to grant me not just forgiveness but healing as well.

After that experience in the confessional, I decided to silently carry this prayer in my heart every time I walked up to receive Communion. After all, isn't the Eucharist the ultimate sign of God's miraculous mercy for us? We all need the mercy of our all-loving God. Years later, when I was seeking healing through therapy, my counselor would remind me of God's "infinite space pit of mercy" that is there just for me . . . just for each of us.

The Jesus Prayer

Lord Jesus Christ, Son of the living God,
have mercy on me, a sinner.

Stolen Moments with Jesus
Kendra Tierney

I believe Jesus Christ is present in the Eucharist in every Catholic church. He is waiting for me, hidden in the tabernacle or exposed in the monstrance. The problem for me is never belief. It's that *he* waits quietly, patiently, not making demands. My children are less subtle in their requests on my time.

It's easy to allow my responsibilities as a wife and mother to fill not only my hands and my days but also my heart and my thoughts. But my vocation to family life is founded on my love of God, so I'm always going to be a better wife and mother when I'm being a better Catholic. My solution for this season of life has been stolen moments with Jesus: a few minutes before the tabernacle after Mass, a stop in the silent church—noisy kids in tow—while running errands, beginning some time with my husband or friends with Jesus in the adoration chapel, and always—*always*—recourse to an Act of Spiritual Communion. I say it at the end of a visit to the Blessed Sacrament (be it long or short), any time I'm driving past a Catholic church and cannot go inside, or when family obligations keep me from daily Mass. It's a reminder of my love for Jesus and his for me, in this and every season of life.

Act of Spiritual Communion

I wish, my Lord, to receive you
With the purity, humility, and devotion
With which your most holy Mother received you
With the spirit and fervor of the saints. Amen.[4]

Or:

My Jesus, I believe that you are present in the Most Holy Sacrament. I love you above all things, and I desire to receive you into my soul. Since I cannot at this moment receive you sacramentally, come at least spiritually into my heart. I embrace you as if you were already there and unite myself wholly to you. Never permit me to be separated from you. Amen.[5]

A Daily Encounter with Mystery

Karianna Frey

"It's Angelus time!" The calls of my children reverberate through the house as our smart speaker chimes the Angelus bells. For just over one minute each day, we pause in our labors, right where we are, to remember the redeeming work of the Lord brought to us through the fiat of one young woman.

While this prayer is traditionally offered three times daily, we make it our goal to pray it at least once each day. Echoing the call-and-response style of our liturgy, the Angelus allows us to enter into the mysteries of the Annunciation, Incarnation, and Passion while at the same time reminding us of our daily call to conversion: to accept God's will in our lives while not fully knowing or understanding what the outcome will be, but trusting all the while that he has it in control.

Mother Mary is more than just a model of motherhood; she is a model of complete trust in the Lord's goodness. She said yes, not knowing how her family and community would react. She said yes, not knowing that she would have to flee to Egypt with her husband and a newborn baby. She said yes, not knowing that she would see her son loved and later rejected by those he came to serve. She said yes, not knowing that one day she would hold the broken body of her son, and she said yes, not knowing that he would rise again and be glorified. She said yes.

Make this antiphonal (alternating) Marian prayer a "holy habit"—a lovely reminder to turn our thoughts to God in the middle of each day!

The Angelus

V. The Angel of the Lord declared unto Mary.

R. And she conceived of the Holy Spirit. *Hail, Mary . . .*

V. Behold the handmaid of the Lord.

R. Be it done unto me according to Thy word. *Hail Mary . . .*

V. And the Word was made Flesh.

R. And dwelt among us. *Hail Mary . . .*

V. Pray for us, O holy Mother of God.

R. That we may be made worthy of the promises of Christ.

V. Let us pray:

Pour forth, we beseech Thee, O Lord, Thy grace into our hearts, that we to whom the Incarnation of Christ Thy Son was made known by the message of an angel, may by His Passion and Cross be brought to the glory of His Resurrection. Through the same Christ Our Lord. Amen.[6]

THE AVE PRAYER BOOK FOR CATHOLIC MOTHERS

A Spiritual Heart Transplant

Emily Jaminet

As mothers, we are called to love from the very depths of our soul. But what about the times we grow weary and overwhelmed? In these moments, Jesus offers us his Most Sacred Heart to be our strength and the fount of all blessings. He desires that we offer our hearts to him so that he can transform our weariness. He desires to make us humble, patient, pure, and wholly obedient to the will of God. This spiritual heart transplant is what we need to love our family and all those we encounter.

The Holy Heart of Jesus wants to be alive in us. He wants to protect us from spiritual and temporal dangers. We are called to abandon ourselves to the Lord and place our trust in his heart, and he will take care of everything.

Most Holy Heart of Jesus Prayer

O most holy Heart of Jesus, fountain of every blessing,
I adore You, I love You, and with a lively sorrow for my sins,
I offer You this poor heart of mine.
Make me humble, patient, pure, and wholly obedient to Your will.
Grant, good Jesus, that I may live in You and for You.
Protect me in the midst of danger; comfort me in my afflictions.
Give me health of body, assistance in my temporal needs,
Your blessing on all that I do, and the grace of a holy death. Amen.[7]

Making a Holy Hour

Susanna Parent

"Be still and know that I am God" (Ps 46). God longs to be with us in the silence. As Cardinal Robert Sarah says, God "drapes himself in silence." This silence can be found in a holy hour of eucharistic adoration. This is a time of prayer with Jesus in the Blessed Sacrament, worshipping him as he is exposed in the monstrance.

Here are a few tips to help you enter into this time of intimacy with the Lord.

1. *Make an act of faith*, acknowledging Jesus' Real Presence before you. Then, enter into the silence with the acronym ARRR: Acknowledge, Relate, Receive, and Resolve.

2. *Acknowledge:* Take a moment to acknowledge your thoughts and feelings, and spend time recognizing what is on your heart and mind. Give God everything.

3. *Relate:* Have a conversation with the Lord. Tell him your sorrows and your joys. Be honest with him about everything you are putting into words.

4. *Receive:* Ask the Lord how he is loving you and what his message is for you. Read slowly and prayerfully a passage of scripture such as Psalm 46 (below), and let his word "drape" over you as you receive it.

5. *Resolve:* Make a resolution based on what the Lord has given you in prayer. This could mean journaling about your experience or offering someone in your life forgiveness and mercy.

Psalm 46

God is our refuge and strength,
a very present help in trouble.
Therefore we will not fear though the earth should change,
  though the mountains shake in the heart of the sea;
though its waters roar and foam,
  though the mountains tremble with its tumult.

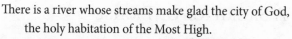

There is a river whose streams make glad the city of God,
  the holy habitation of the Most High.
God is in the midst of her, she shall not be moved;
  God will help her when morning dawns.
The nations rage, the kingdoms totter;
  he utters his voice, the earth melts.
The LORD of hosts is with us;
  the God of Jacob is our refuge.

Come, behold the works of the LORD,
  how he has wrought desolations in the earth.
He makes wars cease to the end of the earth;
  he breaks the bow, and shatters the spear,
  he burns the chariots with fire!
"Be still, and know that I am God.
  I am exalted among the nations,
  I am exalted in the earth!"
The LORD of hosts is with us;
  the God of Jacob is our refuge.

A Sacrifice of Praise

Mary Lenaburg

Walking with me hand in hand, my husband sang the beautiful words of the song below as we accompanied our daughter Courtney out of the church for the last time. Our son was several steps ahead of us, surrounded by his cousins, and had his hand on his sister's casket, clinging to the last moments of having her physical body in our presence. The lyrics poured over me like a healing balm, and I made a conscious effort to praise God in that moment of incredibly deep pain for the blessing of my sweet daughter's life. Tears fell as my heart broke again for the loss of her.

As the choir serenaded my daughter one last time, I struggled to make that sacrifice of praise, yet in that moment all I wanted was to have her back in my arms, no matter the cost. But that was my will, not God's.

The words of this song have become a daily prayer for me since her passing. Lord, let me praise you in the hard and in the easy. Let me praise you in the broken and in the whole. Let me praise you in the light and in the dark. No matter what, may I always make a sacrifice of praise.

O God beyond All Praising

Then hear, O gracious Savior,
accept the love we bring,
that we who know your favor
may serve you as our King;
and whether our tomorrows
be filled with good or ill,
we'll triumph through our sorrows
and rise to bless you still:
to marvel at your beauty
and glory in your ways,
and make a joyful duty
our sacrifice of praise.

COMMUNING WITH CHRIST

Karianna Frey

The Body of Christ dissolves upon my tongue, infusing my body, soul, mind, and spirit, as I kneel in thanksgiving for his freely given gift. I make the Sign of the Cross and begin my prayer of reflection, *"Anima Christi, sanctifica me . . . ."*

The Anima Christi has been a part of my prayer life since my conversion. Part of what drew me to the Church was her rich history, and when I pray the traditional prayers, I am united with the holy men and women who have traveled before me.

While I typically say this prayer after receiving Christ in the Eucharist, to me this is more than a prayer of thanksgiving; it is a prayer of surrender. By the very act of receiving the gift of Christ, I am inviting him to change me from within:

- for his Soul to make my body into a holy dwelling place,
- for his Body to redeem me,
- for his Blood to course through my veins,
- for the water from his pierced side to cleanse me of all of my iniquities,
- for his Passion to strengthen me for the trials to come,
- for his protection from the evil one who seeks to separate us, and
- for perseverance to the end, until he calls me home to praise him forever.

Because that is really what we are created for: to be happy with God in heaven, forever and ever.

Widely attributed to St. Ignatius Loyola (1491–1556), the words of this prayer will lead you deep into the heart of Jesus, whether you say them after receiving Communion or as a morning offering, in which you ask the Lord for a sense of his abiding presence through the day.

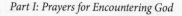

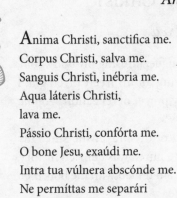

Anima Christi

Anima Christi, sanctifica me.	Soul of Christ, sanctify me.
Corpus Christi, salva me.	Body of Christ, save me.
Sanguis Christi, inébria me.	Blood of Christ, intoxicate me.
Aqua láteris Christi,	Water from the side of Christ,
lava me.	wash me.
Pássio Christi, confórta me.	Suffering of Christ, comfort me.
O bone Jesu, exaúdi me.	O good Jesus, listen to me.
Intra tua vúlnera abscónde me.	Within your wounds hide me.
Ne permíttas me separári	Do not allow me to be separated
a te.	from you.
Ab hoste maligno defénde me.	From the wicked enemy defend me.
In hora mortis meae voca me.	In the hour of my death call me.
Et jube me veníre	And command me to come
ad te	unto you
Ut cum Sanctis tuis	That with your saints I may
laudem te	praise you
In saécula saeculórum.	Into the ages of ages.
Amen.	Amen.[8]

When You Need to Go to Confession

Maurisa Mayerle

I've always struggled with anxiety about how others see me. This extends to worry over what my priest may think of me or how he might admonish me in Confession. That fear has sometimes made me resist or put off going to Confession.

This may seem counterintuitive, but I've overcome this paralyzing fear of the confessional by scheduling the sacrament with my priest, rather than going anonymously. Now, I'm sure many would counsel me to confess to a priest who is a stranger. Here's the thing, though: Knowing that my priest knows my identity has forced me to put that concern aside and acknowledge the truth that he is acting *in persona Christi*. Christ already sees and knows all; I can't hide anything from him. So why should I try to hide the truth from the priest, who only wants me to be free and healed?

It also helps to prepare for Confession. Find a place and time where you can have quiet and solitude. Pray and ask for peace, an awareness of the sins you need to confess, and courage to confess fully and honestly. Use a good examination of conscience—many abound on the internet. I recommend finding one that closely examines the Ten Commandments, the precepts of the Church, and addresses your particular state in life. I find writing out my confession helps me remember everything I want to say and also helps me see patterns that need to be worked on and rooted out.

Before entering the confessional, continue to pray for guidance and the fortitude to confess even the most embarrassing sins. Embrace the truth that the priest, like Jesus, absolutely wants to see you whole. Let go of the fear and worry. Forgiveness, healing, and love are what remain.

Prayer for Courage

Jesus, you are the Physician of Souls, and I know you desire that I be made whole. Please fill me with your peace as I prepare to confess my sins. Help me make a good and thorough examination of conscience and Confession without fear so that I may be healed and filled with your grace. Amen.

Adoring the Heart of Love

Emily Jaminet

In the next section of this book, you will discover a series of litanies —many of them original compositions—that cover a wide spectrum of motherly intentions. Litanies are one of my favorite prayer forms; each line provides an opportunity for reflection. I especially love the Litany of the Sacred Heart of Jesus because it helps me reflect on Jesus' love, his desire to show mercy, and his boundless goodness. Reflecting on these qualities of the heart of our Lord can only make me a more loving, more merciful mother. May this special prayer fill your heart with God's love and transform you from the inside out!.

The response (R) is, *Have mercy on us.*

Litany of the Sacred Heart of Jesus (Abridged)

Lord, have mercy . . . *Lord, have mercy.*
Christ, have mercy . . . *Christ, have mercy.*
Lord, have mercy . . . *Lord, have mercy.*

God our Father in heaven—R
God the Son, Redeemer of the world—R
God the Holy Spirit—R

Heart of Jesus, aflame with love for us—R
Heart of Jesus, source of justice and love—R
Heart of Jesus, full of goodness and love—R
Heart of Jesus, well-spring of all virtues—R
Heart of Jesus, worthy of all praise—R
Heart of Jesus, King and Center of all hearts—R
Heart of Jesus, generous to all who turn to you—R
Heart of Jesus, fount of all life and holiness—R
Heart of Jesus, salvation of all who trust in you—R

Jesus, gentle and humble of heart . . . *touch our hearts and make them like yours.*

Let us pray: Father, we thank you for your Son, the greatest gift in our life. Open our hearts to your love and inspire us to spread that love throughout the earth so to set the world ablaze. Bless us and protect us from all harm. May we dwell forever in the heart of your Son. Jesus, we trust in you. Amen.[9]

Litanies of Our Lives

In the liturgy, a litany is an antiphonal reading (alternating leader and congregation) that draws the people together in a singular intention, along with the Communion of Saints. "The hymns and litanies of the Liturgy of the Hours integrate the prayer of the psalms into the age of the Church, expressing the symbolism of the time of day, the liturgical season, or the feast being celebrated" (*CCC* 1177).

When used in private prayer, as they are here, litanies draw our attention to the attributes of God that are worthy of adoration, and those of the saints that are most worthy of imitation. Chanted or sung, each line becomes a kind of aspiration, breathing out our deepest concerns and breathing in the Spirit, who invigorates and strengthens us. As we read in Ephesians:

> And do not get drunk with wine, for that is debauchery; but be filled with the Spirit, addressing one another in psalms and hymns and spiritual songs, singing and making melody to the Lord with all your heart, always and for everything giving thanks in the name of our Lord Jesus Christ to God the Father (Eph 5:18–20).

Litany of Gratefulness

Sarah Christmyer

This original litany, drawn from Psalm 100, can be used as a morning offering, bedtime examen, or any time you are inspired to thank God for his goodness.

The text of the original psalm is in bold. The response (R) is, *Lord, I am so grateful.*

Make a joyful noise to the Lord, all the lands!
Lord, I lift my heart to you in grateful praise for the gift of motherhood.—R
Serve the Lord with gladness! Come into his presence with singing!
I am grateful for the children you gave me to love, nurture, and guide.—R
Know that the Lord is God! It is he that made us, and we are his;
I am grateful that you formed each one for a specific purpose, and know all their strengths and flaws.—R
We are his people, and the sheep of his pasture.
I am grateful that you love and care for [name(s)] even more than I do.—R

Enter his gates with thanksgiving, and his courts with praise!
When I can be there to comfort and console, to patch up and advise—R
Give thanks to him, bless his name!
For patience and understanding and the ability to forgive—R
For the Lord is good;
For allowing me to share your Cross when they cause me pain, and for the resurrection of joy when I see signs of growth and maturity—R
His mercy endures for ever,
For the example, guidance, and support of your Blessed Mother—R
And his faithfulness to all generations.

Lord, I am so grateful for the love and guidance you have shown me and my family, today and forever. Amen.

Litany for Guidance

Deb Kelsey-Davis

This original prayer, based on Micah 6:8, is an important reminder of the three simple requirements the Father has of his children: to do justice, to love kindness, and to walk humbly with God.

As I begin each day, help me to remember all you require of me is . . .
To do justice, to love kindness, and to walk humbly with our God.
When my patience is strained, and I can't do it all, guide me, Lord . . .
To do justice, to love kindness, and to walk humbly with our God.
When I feel the need to rush in and take control of a situation, guide me, Lord . . .
To do justice, to love kindness, and to walk humbly with our God.
When family members hurt my feelings with their words or actions, guide me, Lord . . .
To do justice, to love kindness, and to walk humbly with our God.
When I feel alone and misunderstood, guide me, Lord . . .
To do justice, to love kindness, and to walk humbly with our God.
For your constant love and mercy I am grateful. Please continue to guide me, Lord . . .
To do justice, to love kindness, and to walk humbly with our God.
With shared laughter and joy please continue to bless me, Lord. Help me . . .
To do justice, to love kindness, and to walk humbly with our God.
For the gift of motherhood, in all its forms, I praise you. Please help me, Lord . . .
To do justice, to love kindness, and to walk humbly with our God.
As day ends, when I fall into bed, reassure me that truly all you require of me is . . .
To do justice, to love kindness, and to walk humbly with our God. Amen.

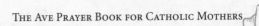

LITANY OF HUMILITY

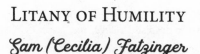

Sam (Cecilia) Fatzinger

Humility is a virtue no mother should ask for out loud; it's like asking for patience. Every mother gets her fair share of humiliating experiences. If you haven't had them yet, they are coming, probably when you least expect it.

Like the time you are working in the church nursery and exclaim over a child who is behaving "that way" . . . then turn around and see your precious little angel push a kid off a chair. Or you wake up to find your "holy" teenager—the altar server, youth group leader, and straight-A student—sneaked out of the house last night to smoke a Juul with some of his friends. That could never happen, right? No—never!

I discovered the Litany of Humility[10] when I was about seventeen years old. A nice lady I worked with at our local pregnancy center gave me an old, traditional prayer book, and I found myself going back repeatedly to the Litany of Humility. Each time I prayed the litany, the virtue I needed most would jump out at me. If you ask Jesus, he'll do it for you, too. Just ask him to grant you the wisdom you need to chip away at any vices and work on these holy virtues to help you become the saint that God created you to be.

When the hidden humiliations of motherhood begin to chafe, this beautiful litany can fortify the soul and bring peace to your heart.

The response is in italics.

O Jesus! meek and humble of heart, *hear me.*
From the desire of being esteemed, *deliver me, Jesus.*
From the desire of being loved, *deliver me, Jesus.*
From the desire of being extolled, *deliver me, Jesus.*
From the desire of being honored, *deliver me, Jesus.*
From the desire of being praised, *deliver me, Jesus.*
From the desire of being preferred to others, *deliver me, Jesus.*
From the desire of being consulted, *deliver me, Jesus.*
From the desire of being approved, *deliver me, Jesus.*

From the fear of being humiliated, *deliver me, Jesus.*
From the fear of being despised, *deliver me, Jesus.*
From the fear of being rebuked, *deliver me, Jesus.*
From the fear of being mocked, *deliver me, Jesus.*
From the fear of being excluded, *deliver me, Jesus.*
From the fear of being ridiculed, *deliver me, Jesus.*
From the fear of being wronged, *deliver me, Jesus.*
From the fear of being suspected, *deliver me, Jesus.*

That others may be loved more than I, *Jesus, grant me the grace to desire it.*
That others may be esteemed more than I, *Jesus, grant me the grace to desire it.*
That, in the opinion of the world, others may increase and I may decrease, *Jesus, grant me the grace to desire it.*
That others may be chosen and I set aside, *Jesus, grant me the grace to desire it.*
That others may be praised and I unnoticed, *Jesus, grant me the grace to desire it.*
That others may be preferred to me in everything, *Jesus, grant me the grace to desire it.*
That others may become holier than I, provided that I may become as holy as I should, *Jesus, grant me the grace to desire it.*

Litany of Joy

Allison Gingras

On a day when joy hung in my heart by a thread, I arrived at the chapel for my holy hour overwhelmed by challenges, obstacles, and burdens. I came with just a pen and pad, ready to take dictation from the Holy Spirit on joy. True joy is a gift from God, something this world cannot give. We often confuse it with happiness, which, as the saying goes, is fleeting. Joy is the hope of heaven, the knowledge of the Father's everlasting love, and a perseverance in faith that roots us in life, often despite our present circumstances.

The antiphonal response (R) is, *May the joy of the Lord fill my heart.*

To see the blessings in every circumstance—R

To embrace the hope only heaven offers—R

To believe in your promise of true peace—R

To rejoice in the Triune God—Father, Son, and Holy Spirit—R

To employ the wisdom that transcends the tangible and visible—R

To seek, knowing I will always find—R

To ask, believing I will always be answered—R

To knock, confident your loving hand will always open the door—R

To bask peacefully in the splendid light of Christ—R

To listen to the whispers of the Lord over the din of the world—R

To sing songs of praise in the storms of life—R

To remain steadfast in faith, hope, and love—R

To trust that nothing can separate me from the love of God—R

And to revel before the Real Presence of Christ in the Eucharist,

Recognizing in each moment a foretaste of what awaits me in heaven—R

Litany of Togetherness

Jaymie Stuart Wolfe

I wrote this litany as a personal reminder to treasure the time I spend with my family, not only during holidays and milestone events, but especially in the daily activities of ordinary life. As children leave home and start families of their own, we may not always be able to gather in person. Remember, too, that God hears our prayers for deliverance from those inner obstacles to togetherness that every family experiences at some time or to some degree.

The responses are in italics.

God, the Father of Heaven, *have mercy on us.*
God the Son, Redeemer of the World, *have mercy on us.*
God the Holy Spirit, *have mercy on us.*
Holy Trinity, One God, *have mercy on us.*

When we are unable to be with each other, *bring us together, Lord.*
When we are pressed for time, *bring us together, Lord.*
When we are financially stressed, *bring us together, Lord.*
When responsibilities keep us apart, *bring us together, Lord.*
When we disagree, *bring us together, Lord.*
When we are separated by circumstances beyond our control, *bring us together, Lord.*
When we are separated by distance or death, *bring us together, Lord.*

From taking each other for granted, *deliver us, Lord.*
From the desire for attention or control, *deliver us, Lord.*
From petty expectations, *deliver us, Lord.*
From the burden of unreasonable demands, *deliver us, Lord.*
From anger and envy, *deliver us, Lord.*
From the fear of judgment or rejection, *deliver us, Lord.*
From misunderstandings and assumptions, *deliver us, Lord.*
From unhappy memories and past hurts, *deliver us, Lord.*
From discord and division, *deliver us, Lord.*

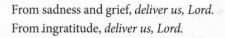

From sadness and grief, *deliver us, Lord.*
From ingratitude, *deliver us, Lord.*

In times of presence, *make us one, Lord.*
In times of absence, *make us one, Lord.*
In times of loneliness, *make us one, Lord.*
In times of joyful celebration, *make us one, Lord.*
In times of illness, *make us one, Lord.*
In times of prosperity and health, *make us one, Lord.*
In times of struggle and difficulty, *make us one, Lord.*
By the bonds of affection, *make us one, Lord.*
By the gift of faith, *make us one, Lord.*
By the power of your love, *make us one, Lord.*
By the waters of Baptism, *make us one, Lord.*
By the grace of forgiveness, *make us one, Lord.*
At the altar of Eucharist, *make us one, Lord.*
In Holy Communion, *make us one, Lord.*

For the gift of family, *thank you, Lord.*
For the joys we've shared together, *thank you, Lord.*
For the sorrows we've faced together, *thank you, Lord.*
For all we've learned from one another, *thank you, Lord.*
For the time we've spent together, *thank you, Lord.*
For the promise of sharing eternity with you and one another,
    thank you, Lord.

Lamb of God, you take away the sins of the world, *spare us, O Lord.*
Lamb of God, you take away the sins of the world, *graciously hear us, O
    Lord.*
Lamb of God, you take away the sins of the world, *have mercy on us.*

Let us pray: Grant to our family, O Lord, the grace of togetherness, especially
in those times and circumstances that prevent us from gathering. Keep us
mindful of the blessings you have given us. Console us in our loneliness.
Direct our hearts always toward love for you and one another. And bring
all our family to your kingdom, so we may live together in the joy of your
salvation for all eternity. Amen.

LITANY OF TRUST

Jenny Uebbing

I was introduced to the Litany of Trust by Sr. Maria Faustina Pia on a retreat with the Sisters of Life, and I've kept a tattered, pocket-sized copy of it in my nightstand ever since. When I pray this litany, it seems to require an almost physical act of the will to escort all my closest companions to the door of my mind: anxiety, restless self-seeking, resentment, fear. . . I don't know if your struggles are similar to mine, but I do know that praying these words can change a heart—even a heart with a shell like granite.

The response for the first part of the litany (R1) is, *Deliver me, Jesus.*

The response for the second part of the litany (R2) is, *Jesus, I trust in You.*

From the belief that I have to earn Your love—R1
From the fear that I am unlovable—R1
From the false security that I have what it takes—R1
From the fear that trusting You will leave me more destitute—R1
From all suspicion of Your words and promises—R1
From the rebellion against childlike dependency on You—R1
From refusals and reluctances in accepting Your will—R1

From anxiety about the future—R1
From resentment or excessive preoccupation with the past—R1
From restless self-seeking in the present moment—R1
From disbelief in Your love and presence—R1
From the fear of being asked to give more than I have—R1
From the belief that my life has no meaning or worth—R1
From the fear of what love demands—R1
From discouragement—R1

That You are continually holding me, sustaining me, loving me—R2
That Your love goes deeper than my sins and failings, and transforms
    me—R2

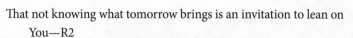

That not knowing what tomorrow brings is an invitation to lean on
  You—R2

That You are with me in my suffering—R2

That my suffering, united to Your own, will bear fruit in this life and the
  next—R2

That You will not leave me orphan, that You are present in Your
  Church—R2

That Your plan is better than anything else—R2

That You always hear me and in Your goodness always respond to me—R2

That You give me the grace to accept forgiveness and to forgive others—R2

That You give me all the strength I need for what is asked—R2

That my life is a gift—R2

That You will teach me to trust You—R2

That You are my Lord and my God—R2

That I am Your beloved one—R2

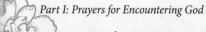

LITANY OF WEAKNESS

Elizabeth Scalia

This original litany offers an opportunity to acknowledge our own faults and failings as well as the infinite strength that is there for the asking. In the words of St. Paul, "For the sake of Christ, then, I am content with weaknesses, insults, hardships, persecutions, and calamities; for when I am weak, then I am strong" (2 Cor 12:10).

The responses are in italics.

Lord, what is before me feels difficult beyond my endurance.
> *But in my weakness, you are my strength; come, Lord Jesus.*

Please be with me in this moment.
> *For in my weakness you are my strength; come, Lord Jesus.*

This feels so heavy, and I fear my own failure.
> *But in my weakness, you are my strength; come, Lord Jesus.*

With so much beyond my control, please show me what I may do.
> *For in my weakness, you are my strength; come, Lord Jesus.*

If a door must now close, give me wisdom to see the open window.
> *For in my weakness, you are my strength; come, Lord Jesus.*

Please lead me from despair and into hope.
> *For in my weakness, you are my strength; come, Lord Jesus.*

Help me to show mercy as I have found mercy in you.
> *For in my weakness, you are my strength; come, Lord Jesus.*

By your Cross, Lord, teach me to trust in God's good purposes.
> *That in my weakness, you are my strength; come, Lord Jesus.*

By your Resurrection, may I live assured by grace that this too shall pass.
> *For in my weakness, you are my strength; come, Lord Jesus.*

Christ Jesus, Alpha and Omega (Rv 1:8), *be my strength.*
Christ Jesus, in whom all things hold together (Col 1:17), *be my strength.*
Christ Jesus, Reconciler of all things (Col 1:19–20), *be my strength.*
Amen.

PART II

PRAYERS FOR GETTING TO KNOW MARY

᚜᚜᚛᚛

"Behold, your mother!"
John 19:27

W hether you are a lifelong Catholic or are fairly new to the faith, Jesus wants you to have a relationship with his mother. Just as he honored Mary throughout his life, entrusting her from the Cross to his beloved disciple—and, by extension, to all of us—so we honor her, not as a goddess, but as our spiritual mother.

Honoring Mary in no way diminishes our relationship with God. In the words of St. Louis de Montfort, "God desires to reveal and show forth Mary, the masterpiece of his hands, in these end times: because she hid herself in the world and made herself less than the dust by her profound humility, having obtained from God, from his apostles and evangelists, that she would not be made manifest at all; and because, since she is the masterpiece of God's hands as much here below by grace as in heaven by glory, he desires to be glorified and praised in her on earth by the living."[1]

The prayers and reflections in this section are intended to help you "go deeper" with Mary, to see her in a new light and to experience her loving concern in a new way. From the familiar prayers of the Rosary to the many Marian devotions that have kept her children close to her throughout history, you can turn to this section any time you feel the need for a little extra motherly tender loving care.

An Introduction to Mary

Heidi Hess Saxton

He was almost three years old the first time I held my son in my arms. Late at night, in the creaky old rocker I'd set up in the corner of his room, I would rock and hum a settling tune and wait with the patience of Job . . . and slowly, furtively, he would slip out of bed and creep over to me, then pat my lap to be let up for a snuggle.

During the daylight hours, he would hide under tables and raise an angry fist if anyone tried to touch him. He wanted his mother, and I wasn't her. He wanted his brother, his father, his toys, and they had all disappeared. But in the night, he was bound and determined he would not lose "the Mommy" too. So he held on tight.

That's the way you've been with Mary, a little voice inside my head chided one night. And in an instant, I understood. This was exactly the way I'd treated her, as a new Catholic—most of the time ignoring her entirely, turning to her only when the night came and there was no one else. But like a good mother, she never gave up on me. And when I became a mother, overnight, to a sibling group of scared and angry little kids, I finally started to get it: Mothers love. They don't need permission. And that love is never wasted.

Blessed One

What was it like for you, Mary?
To hear the shout and feel the stirrings of new life?
You had done nothing but obey, and yet
Weren't you a little embarrassed, all the same?
Did Joseph's anguish and the neighbor's clucking
Ever make you wish you'd been less blessed?

"Blessed are you!" your cousin exclaimed.
"Hail, Graceful One," the angel's voice echoed
In that holy chamber, in your very soul.
At that moment, did you imagine the day
When God's most tender, eternal hope
Would spring forth from your loving arms?

O Blessed Virgin, lead me to Jesus, the source of your purity—and mine. The choices you made were not easy ones. Pray for me, that I might find the courage to do what is right, even when it is the hardest choice to make. May your son always find a soft and welcoming place in my heart. Amen.[2]

The Dominican (Traditional) Rosary

Whether you count the prayers on your fingers or on your grandmother's cherished antique beads, the soothing prayers of the Rosary nourish a mother's soul and provide a strong line of defense in difficult times. The earliest versions of these knotted prayer strings go back to the Desert Fathers of the third century. The version we pray today is traditionally attributed to St. Dominic early in the thirteenth century. The gentle cadence of these familiar prayers leads us to contemplate the lives of Mary and Jesus, and invokes the powerful intercession of the Blessed Mother, the Queen of All Saints.

It can take some time to turn this devotion into a holy habit. I had been a confirmed Catholic for almost a decade when I picked up my beads in earnest, at a time when I was struggling to keep things together in nearly every part of my life. I soon discovered that the power of the Rosary lay not in how smooth or unbroken my recitation, but in how open my heart was to receiving the graces the Lord had for me. By honoring Jesus and his mother and contemplating their earthly life together, I found my own burden grow immeasurably lighter, knowing that I have a mother who continues to pray for me from heaven.

The beginning of this section contains the prayers of the traditional Rosary. After you are comfortable with this version of the devotion, you may want to try one of the other variations at the end of the section—the Franciscan Crown or the scriptural Rosary. For now, grab your beads and listen to the stories of Catholic women like you who want to share why each of these prayers is so meaningful to them. Which set of mysteries do you most need to ponder today?

If you need step-by-step directions on how to use the rosary beads, a free downloadable is available at AveMariaPress.com.

The Sign of the Cross

Rebecca Frech

When I was a little girl, I was terrified of vampires. And monsters. And the dark. And anything that might go bump in the night. I had an older brother who loved scary stories and scaring people, and I was his unhappy audience.

The fall that I turned eight, my mother sent me to stay for a week at my grandparents' house while she organized and packed us up for yet another move. (We were United States Navy people, and moving was a way of life.) My mom, who was usually very thorough, forgot to pack in my suitcase the nightlight that scared away monsters, so that first night, when my grandpa turned off the lights, I began to howl in fear. He ripped the lights on and listened to my tales of nightmares that might be under the bed. He nodded gently and then told me to make the Sign of the Cross.

"It is the most powerful prayer," he said. "It calls on the protection of all three persons of God, and blesses your body in their names. How big you make that cross is how much of yourself you've blessed, so never be ashamed to make a big one. It is an ancient sign of the Trinity, and no demon or monster can stand in the face of such a powerful truth. They run away from it as fast as they can."

With that, he kissed my forehead and turned out the light. I made the biggest cross I could, while still under the covers, from forehead to hipbone, and shoulder to shoulder. Fully blessed and covered with divine favor, I dropped off to sleep.

The Sign of the Cross is one of the most ancient forms of Christian prayer and can be traced back at least to the third century in the teachings of St. Cyprian. It is distinctively Catholic, a sacramental and a sign of our identification with the Passion and Death of the Lord.

By beginning each Rosary with the Sign of the Cross, we affirm that the Rosary is a profoundly Christ-centered prayer that draws us to contemplate the mysteries of the earthly life of the Word made flesh, through the eyes of his mother.

The Sign of the Cross

As you say these words, slowly and reverently
touch your right hand to your forehead and navel,
then left shoulder to right, in the shape of a large cross.

In the name of the Father, and the Son, and the Holy Spirit. Amen.

THE APOSTLES' CREED

Pat Gohn

I learned to pray the Apostles' Creed by heart in my late twenties when I began praying the Rosary more frequently. In time, the Rosary became a daily prayer habit. Our Mother Mary has assisted me in learning about our faith through the mysteries of the Rosary. (They are called "mysteries" not because they are mysterious or unknowable, but precisely because they are the truths that God has *revealed* to us.)

The Rosary is rooted in the central mystery of our faith and Christian life, that is, the Holy Trinity. God loves us so much that he revealed himself to us as Father, Son, and Holy Spirit. As we profess this *Credo*, its twelve short articles describe each member of the Trinity and God's loving plan for us. Ultimately, union with the Trinity is our endgame! Yes—another big reveal—the promise of heaven is true! But until then, we're practicing our faith and, hopefully, professing it with ever-growing vigor and deepening belief.

Summarizing our faith as we begin the Rosary makes perfect sense. And I find the wisdom of a fourth-century bishop, St. Ambrose, inspiring in unpacking the Creed's meaning for our lives: "This Creed is the spiritual seal, our heart's meditation and an ever-present guardian; it is, unquestionably, the treasure of our soul" (*CCC* 197).

The Apostles' Creed

I believe in God,
the Father Almighty,
Creator of heaven and earth,
and in Jesus Christ, his only Son, our Lord,
who was conceived by the Holy Spirit,
born of the Virgin Mary,
suffered under Pontius Pilate,
was crucified, died, and was buried;
he descended into hell;
on the third day he rose again from the dead;
he ascended into heaven,
and is seated at the right hand of God the Father Almighty;

from there he will come to judge the living and the dead.
I believe in the Holy Spirit,
the Holy Catholic Church,
the Communion of Saints,
the forgiveness of sins,
the resurrection of the body,
and life everlasting.
Amen.

THE OUR FATHER
Rachel Bulman

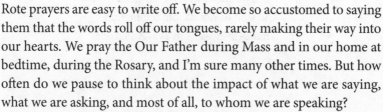

Rote prayers are easy to write off. We become so accustomed to saying them that the words roll off our tongues, rarely making their way into our hearts. We pray the Our Father during Mass and in our home at bedtime, during the Rosary, and I'm sure many other times. But how often do we pause to think about the impact of what we are saying, what we are asking, and most of all, to whom we are speaking?

"Our Father." While most of us immediately think of the intimacy suggested by the word "father," I find that my attention is arrested by the possessive noun, "our." As Jesus is teaching this prayer in the Gospel of Matthew, he doesn't direct the disciples to pray with words that denote personal ownership ("My Father"), but instead invites them to use the words of familial relationship. The words "Our Father" unite us not only with God himself but with the others that are sharing in this prayer all over the world.

For mothers, wading through days that are monotonous and stressful, even praying can often seem lonely. But discovering the "our" in this prayer unites me with every other person that utters the same words. It's no longer me reaching out only for the Father, but it's also me reaching out for others through him.

Pondering this prayer, I am also riveted to the lines about forgiveness. Motherhood is never easy, and ultimately, unforgiveness wounds us. I am not speaking only of forgiving others but forgiving ourselves, too. *No one mothers like you.* Even our frailties, misgivings, and missteps can be transformed into something beautiful when given to our Father. He loves you so much that he has invited you to be a co-creator with him, to mother with him. And every day, an example of this love of God calls you "mom."

The Our Father

Our Father, who art in heaven,
hallowed be Thy name.
Thy kingdom come
Thy will be done

on earth as it is in heaven.
Give us this day our daily bread;
and forgive us our trespasses
as we forgive those who trespass against us.
And lead us not us into temptation,
but deliver us from evil. Amen.

THE HAIL MARY

Sarah A. Reinhard

The Hail Mary has been my comfort prayer for as many years as I have been Catholic. Like the blankies my children trail around the house, clinging to their worn-soft and faded scraps of fabric, the Hail Mary has become the way I cling to Mama Mary's skirt. When my heart aches, when I need to be held, when I'm worried or troubled, the words I can't find on my own shape themselves into a Hail Mary. I pray it instinctively, the way my children grab my hand without even knowing it when we're walking side by side.

When I don't know the words for the desires of my heart, when I'm lonely or sad or just at odds with the world, I can lean into the Hail Mary, finding in the words so many spiritual delights as they lead me closer to Mary's son.

Over the years, I've prayed the Hail Mary quickly and slowly, barely thinking and also reflecting on every word. Rooted in both scripture and tradition, this prayer has become a beacon in my spiritual life. May it guide you, as it has me, closer to Jesus through Mary.

The Hail Mary

Hail Mary, full of grace, the Lord is with thee.
Blessed art thou among women,
and blessed is the fruit of thy womb, Jesus.
Holy Mary, Mother of God, pray for us sinners,
now and at the hour of our death. Amen.

The Glory Be

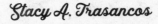

Whenever I say this short prayer, I think of the big bang and thank God for my children.

Glory be to the Father, the source, the originator, the first principle of all things. The Father communicates all of himself to the Son, kind of like when my husband stared at our newborn son, and I knew he would pour everything he's got into that child.

Glory be to the Son, who proceeds from the Father as an act of generation, a conception, analogous in human experience to the procession or generation of the intellect when the mind expresses itself in a concept—the Word, Rationality Itself.

Glory be to the Holy Spirit, who proceeds from the Father and the Son as one, breathed forth in an act of free and good will—the Advocate, Love Itself.

God made the whole universe with this perfect thinking and willing. We humans, made in the image and likeness of God, stand here every day, able to think and will, our hearts beating with more precise chemical equations than any scientist can ever hope to write down.

A baby is a creature God shaped into being, a co-creator. Our daughters will move a great many atoms. Our sons will innovate. And no matter how hard life gets—and life can be very hard—all I ever have to do is look up at the stars where all the elements come from, and I can know with certainty that in the end, life will go everlastingly on if I pray for the grace in each moment to unite my will to God's. There *will always be* reason and love, just as it was in the beginning.

The Glory Be

Glory be to the Father,
And to the Son,
And to the Holy Spirit.
As it was in the beginning, is now,
And ever shall be,
World without end. Amen.

The Fatima Prayer

Maria Morera Johnson

The Fatima Prayer, traditionally prayed at the end of each decade of the Rosary, expresses much about our Catholic faith. At its core, it is a prayer of both forgiveness and mercy. Sometimes I find myself praying it at random times during the day.

- *O my Jesus*—speaks to a sweet, childlike adoration of the Lord
- *forgive us our sins*—begs for forgiveness, together, all of us
- *save us from the fires of hell*—acknowledges what awaits sinners
- *lead all souls to heaven*—speaks to our longing to join Jesus in heaven
- *especially those most in need of thy mercy*—including those who have no one else to pray for them

This brief but powerful prayer comes to us from the children to whom an angel and the Blessed Mother appeared in Fatima, Portugal, in 1917. The three children—Lucia, and brother and sister Jacinta and Francisco (now canonized saints)—received messages first from the angel, and then from the Blessed Mother herself.

During these appearances, the children learned of great trials to come, and the importance of praying the Rosary daily for peace in the world and for the conversion of sinners. Our Lady of Fatima instructed the children to add this prayer to the holy Rosary. The Blessed Mother also urged the children to pray the Rosary daily and spread the devotion to others.

Our Lady of Fatima, pray for us.

The Fatima Prayer

O my Jesus, forgive us our sins.
Save us from the fires of hell.
Lead all souls to heaven,
especially those most in need of thy mercy. Amen.

The Hail Holy Queen

Leticia Ochoa Adams

It was April of 2016 when I experienced the power of the Hail Holy Queen. I was sitting next to the hospital bed of my uncle, Tío Roy as he was dying; his wife, my aunt, Tía Mary, was leading me and my cousins in a Rosary.

My entire life Mary had been in the background, silently watching over me. She never imposed herself, never judged; she just stayed close, hoping and praying that one day I would find my way back to her son. Watching the man who had protected me my entire life die, I followed Tía in the prayers of the Rosary, wanting to thank them both for always being there for me.

Ten months later, Tía would be gone; a month after her death, my oldest son Anthony died by suicide. During that awful time, the Hail Holy Queen was the only prayer that I could pray: As Mother of Mercy, she was exactly the mother I needed in my grief. Again, I could feel Mary in the background praying for me and hoping that I pulled through to the other side of my depression and guilt after Anthony's suicide. She was and is my peace, my place of comfort.

With Mary, I can be me with my pain and heartbreak. The Hail Holy Queen reminds me that I am in the presence of the Mother of God, who knows the pain of losing a son.

The Hail Holy Queen

Hail, Holy Queen, Mother of mercy,
Our life, our sweetness, and our hope!
To thee do we cry, poor banished children of Eve.
To thee do we send up our sighs,
Mourning and weeping in this valley of tears.
Turn then, O most gracious Advocate, thine eyes of mercy toward us;
And after this our exile, show unto us the blessed fruit of thy womb, Jesus.
O clement, O loving, O sweet Virgin Mary.
V: Pray for us, O holy Mother of God,
R: That we may be made worthy of the promises of Christ.

Let us pray: O God, whose only begotten Son, by his life, death, and resurrection, has purchased for us the rewards of eternal life, grant, we beseech Thee, that meditating on these mysteries of the most holy Rosary of the Blessed Virgin Mary, we may imitate what they contain, and obtain what they promise, through the same Christ our Lord. Amen.

The Joyful Mysteries

Luz Torres

The Joyful Mysteries of the Rosary are traditionally offered on Mondays and Saturdays, and they draw us back to the great mystery of the Incarnation—God becoming man in order to reunite Creator and creation. The mysteries include:

1. *The Annunciation*: The angel proclaims the Incarnation to Mary. We pray for the grace to say yes to God, even when we do not fully understand what is ahead.
2. *The Visitation*: Mary shares her joy with Elizabeth. We pray for the courage to share what God has done for us with family and friends.
3. *The Nativity*: The birth of Jesus in Bethlehem. We pray for those who are far from home, that they would find loving welcome among us.
4. *The Presentation*: Mary and Joseph bring Jesus to the Temple and meet Simeon and Anna. We pray for the faith to see the hand of God at work in his Church.
5. *The Finding of Jesus in the Temple*: Mary and Joseph discover Jesus in the Temple after losing him for three days. We pray for the grace to persevere when God seems far away.

"Hail, full of grace . . . . "

As I ponder the moment when the angel Gabriel appeared to Mary, I can only imagine how afraid she must have been in the face of uncertainty. Can you imagine experiencing this? Being told, "You will conceive in your womb and bear a son, and you shall call his name Jesus" (Lk 1:31)?

There are many annunciation moments in our lives—sometimes joyful, sometimes sorrowful—when we find ourselves afraid to say yes and fully trust in that decision. I personally connect with the Joyful Mysteries because at a very young age I was told I was expecting and, like Mary, I did not know what was in store for me. Despite my fear, I placed all my trust in our heavenly mother Mary, knowing that she would protect and guide me along the way.

As you reflect on the Joyful Mysteries, open your heart to that moment when Mary said yes to God. Ask Mary to guide you in saying yes to whatever the Lord has in store for you. She will give you peace in your heart, strength to bear your cross, and the joy to believe and stay hopeful.

THE SORROWFUL MYSTERIES

Sherry Antonetti

Traditionally offered on Tuesdays and Fridays, the Sorrowful Mysteries of the Rosary are a beloved source of consolation and healing in times of adversity and sorrow, when our cross seems heavy. These mysteries include:

1. *The Agony in the Garden*: Jesus prays in Gethsemane with his disciples. We pray for those who feel isolated and abandoned in their sorrow.
2. *The Scourging at the Pillar*: Pilate has Jesus beaten bloody by the Roman soldiers. We pray for the innocent suffering all around the world.
3. *The Crowning with Thorns*: The soldiers mock Jesus as a pretend king. We pray for those bearing the burden of mental or emotional illness.
4. *The Carrying of the Cross*: Jesus falls beneath the load of the Cross, and Simon of Cyrene is pressed into service. We pray for caregivers, first responders, and all those entrusted with the task of accompanying the suffering.
5. *The Crucifixion*: Jesus dies between two criminals, forgiving those who are responsible and commending his spirit to his Father. We pray for those who are facing death with the added burden of regret and guilt, that they would turn to God for pardon and mercy.

Every time we suffer or are asked to share in the sufferings of someone else, we're offered the opportunity to enter into the Sorrowful Mysteries. We commiserate with Jesus in his agony in the garden when we feel overwhelmed by our trials. We feel the mockery and scourging of the world when we choose to be faithful to Christ rather than to worldly ideals. We endure the thorns of our thoughts, temptations that bore into the heart and cause pain.

We've all known the burden of carrying our cross, or of assisting another in the carrying of theirs. Eventually, we all wind up at the foot of the Cross of Jesus. There we can give all our trials and sins and troubles to Christ, or run away from the Cross and the means by which all our sufferings are redeemed.

I've been given this special opportunity to enter into the Sorrowful Mysteries by accompanying loved ones in their sufferings: my father's Alzheimer's, my son's Down syndrome, and my husband's cancer. I've also experienced firsthand the loneliness of estrangement from family. In each case, the answer is always the same: Enter into the Sorrowful Mysteries. Leave it all at the Cross. Mary is there with us, and in God's perfect time it will be healed . . . all of it.

The Luminous Mysteries

Lisa M. Hendey

Traditionally offered on Thursdays, the Luminous Mysteries of the Rosary (the "Mysteries of Light") were recommended to us by St. John Paul II in his 2002 apostolic letter *Rosarium Virginis Mariae*. The Luminous Mysteries describe the significant moments in "Christ's public ministry between his Baptism and his Passion."[3] Expanding the traditional Rosary by incorporating these mysteries makes it a "compendium of the Gospel." These mysteries include:

1. *The Baptism of Jesus*: Jesus is baptized by his cousin John in the Jordan. We pray for those still wandering in darkness, that they might discover the Light of the World.
2. *The Wedding Feast at Cana*: Jesus performs his first public miracle, turning water to wine. We pray for a renewed understanding of the gift of marriage as a sign of hope and generous, life-giving love.
3. *The Proclamation of the Kingdom*: Jesus preaches the Sermon on the Mount. We pray for those who proclaim the Gospel, that their words would fall on ears ready to embrace the truth.
4. *The Transfiguration*: Jesus takes his disciples up the mountain, where they see his divinity. We pray for believers around the world facing persecution simply for being followers of Jesus, that they would have strength to persevere in faith.
5. *The Institution of the Eucharist*: Jesus offers his Body and Blood at the Last Supper. We pray that eyes would be opened and hearts transformed by the Real Presence of Christ and the graces of the Eucharist.

My lifelong affection for the Rosary deepened exponentially when St. John Paul II gifted us the Luminous Mysteries. Praying with them invites me to unite myself more fully to significant moments in Jesus' public ministry, but also to purposefully embrace challenging moments in my own vocation. Pondering the Baptism of Jesus reminds me, as a mom and mother-in-law, to serve as a trusted light for my children that they might know God's love more deeply. Reflecting on the Wedding Feast at Cana, the gospel passage proclaimed at our nuptial Mass, bonds me to my husband, Greg, as together we embrace God's unique calling for our marriage. Daily, we strive in word and deed to proclaim the Gospel as Jesus did in his Sermon on the Mount. Along this winding path, we're called to bear witness to Jesus' Transfiguration by transforming our own lives in service to others. But how do we accomplish all of this amidst the hardships, busyness, and burdens of family life? Through Christ's gift of the Eucharist, we are fueled, we give thanks, and we are sent out into the world to answer God's call to a life of joy, mission, and love.

THE GLORIOUS MYSTERIES

Christy Isinger

Traditionally offered on Sundays and Wednesdays, the Glorious Mysteries can be seen as the prophetic mysteries of the Rosary. The life of Mary, the first Christian and icon of the Church, hints at the destiny of every believer. In the words of St. Paul, "The saying is sure: If we have died with him [in baptism], we shall also live with him; if we endure, we shall also reign with him" (2 Tm 2:11–12).

1. *The Resurrection*: The women find the tomb empty, and the angel tells them Jesus is risen. We pray for those who are grieving a heavy loss, that the hope of the Resurrection would be theirs.
2. *The Ascension*: Jesus miraculously ascends to heaven before the disciples' eyes. We remember those who have died and are making their journey toward God, especially those in purgatory who have no one to pray for them.
3. *The Descent of the Holy Spirit*: The disciples are empowered at Pentecost, as Jesus promised. We pray for a renewal of the Church and her leaders, that the Holy Spirit would move among God's people in a new way.
4. *The Assumption of Mary*: Mary is taken, body and soul, to heaven. We pray for the grace of perseverance, that we would love God so perfectly that we die ready for heaven.
5. *The Coronation*: Mary is crowned Queen of Heaven, to intercede for us with all the saints and angels. We thank God for the invisible world of saints and angels who continuously intercede for us.

I remember the long, drawn-out days of the last trimester of pregnancy when I was consoled by the repetition of the Joyful Mysteries. The Luminous Mysteries, focused on the Lord's earthly ministry, kept me close to Jesus as I took up the challenges of motherhood. And when praying for family members in their last days, I found that the Sorrowful Mysteries led me to a deeper understanding of how Mary ministers to us as we approach death. Then there are the Glorious Mysteries. To be honest, I have trouble relating them to my very human and earthly life. I have not witnessed an ascension into heaven, or seen fiery tongues descend on the heads of people hidden in a musty upstairs room. And the last two mysteries (the Assumption and the Coronation) aren't even explicitly mentioned in the Bible.

On the other hand, maybe that is why they are called "mysteries." I want the kind of faith that makes room for God to work in ways that I can't always anticipate, or even understand. I want a transforming faith that leaves room for the miraculous. I want to have the faith of Mary, who was willing to believe in something she could not see, could not explain.

As I ponder the miraculous that Mary experienced, as encapsulated in the Glorious Mysteries of the Rosary, I realize what has been entrusted to me. What a beautiful gift to contemplate the miraculous, to meditate on the infinite power of God that has moved and acted in our ordinary world.

A Hymn Prayer

Stephanie A. Sibal

Sr. Helen was my second-grade teacher at St. Anthony School in Winsted, Connecticut. There were many things I adored about her, but she left me with one lesson I still reflect on decades later: *Singing is a form of prayer.*

My parents encouraged music in our home. I played flute, and my younger sister and brother tried various instruments. My father had a beautiful voice, and I have vivid memories of him singing traditional hymns such as "How Great Thou Art" along with our very animated cantor during Mass. Dad's favorite song was Schubert's "Ave Maria." It sends chills down my spine every time I hear that lovely prayer.

I shared Sr. Helen's message with my sons as they grew—and tried to instill in them that music is a gift from God. My oldest, Steven, sang a solo called "Christmas Prayer" in his third-grade Christmas program. He also learned to play the piano and organ. My youngest, Alex, is an accomplished clarinetist and plays multiple instruments.

I selected "Immaculate Mary" as my song-prayer because I recall singing it each year as we celebrated the May Crowning in the grotto at St. Anthony's. But there are so many songs that put prayer in my heart—"On Eagle's Wings," "Laudate Dominum," "Jesus Christ Is Risen Today," "Gather Us In," "O Holy Night." It doesn't matter whether you have perfect pitch or can't carry a tune—God wants you to lift up your voice to him in song.

Immaculate Mary

Immaculate Mary, your praises we sing.
You reign now in heaven with Jesus our King.
Ave, Ave, Ave, Maria! Ave, Ave, Maria!

In heaven the blessed your glory proclaim;
On earth we your children invoke your fair name.
Ave, Ave, Ave, Maria! Ave, Ave, Maria!

We pray for our Mother, the Church upon earth,
And bless, Holy Mary, the land of our birth.
Ave, Ave, Ave, Maria! Ave, Ave, Maria![4]

Praise of a Motherly Heart

Andi Oney

God had a huge plan for the young girl to ponder. Mary was a virgin, not yet married, when the Word became flesh in her womb. She was still pondering the surprise of the Annunciation and the reality of her selfless fiat as she ran to see her older relative, Elizabeth, who had been healed of infertility. As these expectant mothers exchanged prophetic words of encouragement, the encounter had "miracle" written all over it!

Mary's heart sang aloud a love song in praise to God, her words revealing that she was a woman steeped in scripture. She is mother and model for all of us, at every age and stage. We can entrust ourselves to her motherly heart as women in the "Army of Moms," imitating her in the spontaneity of her praise, her trust in God's promises, and her confidence in the prophecy that all generations would call her blessed.

As mothers, we often have innovative prayer lives: praying a Hail Mary while changing a diaper, pleading the blood of Jesus over wayward children, praying the Rosary in carpool, or holding the sacred memories of aged parents who no longer remember. Let's face it, life gets complicated, but in the midst of all the busyness of being a mom, we can ask Mary to help shape our hearts and pray with her, "The Lord has done great things for me, and holy is his name."

The Magnificat

And Mary said,
"My soul magnifies the Lord,
and my spirit rejoices in God my Savior,
for he has regarded the low estate of his handmaiden.
For behold, henceforth all generations will call me blessed;
for he who is mighty has done great things for me,
and holy is his name.
And his mercy is on those who fear him
from generation to generation.
He has shown strength with his arm,
he has scattered the proud in the imagination of their hearts,

he has put down the mighty from their thrones,
and exalted those of low degree;
he has filled the hungry with good things,
and the rich he has sent empty away.
He has helped his servant Israel,
in remembrance of his mercy,
as he spoke to our fathers,
to Abraham and to his posterity for ever."

(Luke 1:46–55)

Praying for the Heart of Mary

Katie Warner

I first stumbled across a shortened version of this lovely prayer of St. Teresa of Calcutta years ago in Fr. Michael Gaitley's *33 Days to Morning Glory*, during my preparation for consecration to Our Lady. It began with five simple words—"Mary, give me your heart"—that quickly became one of my favorite prayers.

I pray it throughout the day whenever I pass the image of the Immaculate Heart of Mary that adorns the wall at the foot of the stairs.

I pray it in moments of frustration or anytime I recognize that my heart doesn't want to be patient, loving, or kind.

I pray it when I need to be long-suffering, self-sacrificing, exceedingly generous, or understanding.

I pray it because even if my heart doesn't want those things, Mary's heart always does. So I implore her to *give me* her always-virtuous heart, attitude, and way of being.

Though I generally pray only those five words—"Mary, give me your heart"—the rest of the prayer is equally powerful for us as mothers. The more we conform our hearts to Our Lady's—the more she gives us her very heart, an undeserved gift stemming from a mother's love—the more we become pure tabernacles, ready to receive our Lord and his will for our lives with total trust and abandonment, as she did.

And then we can love Christ as Mary loves him. And we can serve him by serving others, in the nitty-gritty details and during ordinary days, loving him through the "poor" in our own homes, families, and communities.

Prayer of St. Teresa of Calcutta

Mary, my dearest mother, give me your heart:
so beautiful, so pure, so immaculate,
your heart so full of love and humility,
that I may be able to receive Jesus in the Bread of Life,
love him as you loved him,
and serve him in the distressing disguise of the poorest of the poor.[5]

CALM FOR THE FEARFUL HEART

Kelly M. Wahlquist

There may not be a universal word for it, but there is undoubtedly a feeling we all share the moment we look in our rearview mirror and see red flashing lights. A pleading prayer almost always accompanies that gut-wrenching feeling of panic: "Please don't let those lights be for me!"

When I was growing up, whenever we saw the flashing lights of an ambulance, my grandma instantly prayed out loud. Hers was not a self-serving prayer, but a heartfelt request imploring protection and help for a stranger. This loving mother of eight turned with complete confidence to the most loving of mothers, appealing to her to come to the aid of those in need. It always amazed me to hear my gentle grandma who quietly prayed her Rosary suddenly burst into audible prayer with conviction in her voice—as if she knew Our Lady would hear and answer her plea.

By the age of four, I prayed the Memorare with certitude in my voice whenever I saw flashing lights. At the age of forty, I learned about the "flying novena" of St. Teresa of Calcutta—how she would pray this prayer ten times in quick succession for her most urgent needs, nine times for her intention and once in thanksgiving for the answer sure to come. I realized that both these beautiful women had learned an important spiritual principle: If you need graces fast, you can be confident the Mother of the Word Incarnate will deliver.

The Memorare

Remember, O most gracious Virgin Mary, that never was it known that anyone who fled to thy protection, implored thy help, or sought thine intercession was left unaided.

Inspired by this confidence, I fly unto thee, O Virgin of virgins, my mother; to thee do I come, before thee I stand, sinful and sorrowful. O Mother of the Word Incarnate, despise not my petitions, but in thy mercy hear and answer me. Amen.

When Family Is Far Away

Maria Morera Johnson

A few years ago, I was reunited with family in Cuba I hadn't seen in fifty years. The emotional pain of two political exiles, one from the Spanish Civil War in the 1930s and another from Cuba during the Communist Revolution, had scattered my family across two continents and three countries.

The reunion was beautiful. The surprise that should not have been surprising, the warmth and love we shared even though we hardly knew each other beyond names and pictures, touched me deeply. How was this possible? How did we sit down for meals and chatter away, sharing stories of our lives in the intimate way only family can?

I attribute this ease with one another to the faith that held my nuclear family together and to the source of that example, my grandparents, who through their experience modeled what familial love can be despite physical distance and the hardships that come with it. Prayer was, and continues to be, the bridge that crosses oceans to unite our hearts. I'm certain that my great-grandparents prayed for their children and grandchildren and that, in turn, my grandparents and parents prayed for my generation. I know this because I saw and experienced it.

Prayer is what made my happy reconnection with family a reunion, not a meeting. Prayer is what gives me hope today as our family continues to grow with new generations while jobs and opportunities continue to scatter us across the country. It remains a strong bridge that unites our hearts across the miles.

Prayer to Our Lady of Charity

Good and gracious Lord, I praise you and love you. Thank you for the many graces in my life, especially the beautiful gift of my loving family. Blessed Virgin Mary, Our Lady of Charity, magnify our love for your son. Keep our family faithful. Although our life's journey takes us to new places far and wide, pray for us. Keep us safe from harm. Protect us from evil. And keep our love for the Lord and each other burning in our hearts. Amen.

Let Her Sorrows Pierce Your Heart

Rachel Bulman

The Chaplet of the Seven Sorrows, sometimes called the Servite Rosary, is dedicated to the Seven Sorrows of the Immaculate Heart of Mary. Our Lady of Sorrows is often depicted with a tear-stained face and seven long knives or daggers piercing her heart. You can adapt traditional rosary beads to pray this chaplet, or you can use the chaplet beads designed specifically for the Servite Rosary. Announce each of the sorrows on the large beads, then say an Our Father and seven Hail Marys while meditating on that sorrow, using the scriptural passages provided below. Say "Virgin Most Sorrowful, pray for us" at the end of each decade.

Chaplet of the Seven Sorrows

The First Sorrow: Mary hears the Prophecy of Simeon (Lk 2:34–35).
The Second Sorrow: Mary flees into Egypt with Jesus and Joseph (Mt 2:13–18).
The Third Sorrow: Mary and Joseph seek the child Jesus lost in Jerusalem (Lk 2:41–51).
The Fourth Sorrow: Mary meets Jesus on the Via Dolorosa (Lk 23:27).
The Fifth Sorrow: Mary stands beneath the Cross of her crucified son (Jn 19:18, 25–27).
The Sixth Sorrow: Mary receives the body of her son from the Cross (Mk 15:43–46).
The Seventh Sorrow: Mary witnesses the burial of Jesus in a borrowed tomb (Jn 19:41–42).

Let us pray:

Our Lady of Sorrows, from the utterance of Simeon's dire prophecy regarding your infant son to the final glimpse of your son's linen-wrapped body laid in the tomb of Joseph of Arimathea, each moment of your life was a moment of letting go, of your heart being softened to the point of piercing to allow all of humankind to pass through. Each of your sorrows was part of your mission to be in your very person the Church, bound to both Christ's Mystical and physical body, and destined in your perfect union with him to become the mother of all Christians. Our Lady of Sorrows, pray for us your children, that we would offer our sorrows each day to the Father, in union with your most beloved son. Queen of Sorrows, pray for us.

It may seem rather odd to devote ourselves to a sorrowful mother. How does one find solace in a being so seemingly full of woe? But as with all things Marian, in this mode Mary of Nazareth continues to personify the perfection of humanity for us. Mary's sorrowful, Immaculate Heart is a shining mirror of the Sacred Heart she loved so completely, from the first moment of her unconditional and unrestrained yes to God. Her sorrow does not diminish or weaken her personhood or undermine her mission. Instead, her sorrows highlight the profundity of her call as Mother, as Theotokos, and as the Help of Christians.

The sorrows of Mary are a point of departure for each of us, to choose at each step whether our hearts will remain open and receptive, or closed and hard. These heavy events in Mary's life remind us that she can relate to everything we have suffered: leaving our homes, losing track of our children, watching our beloved ones suffer or even die, and more. Sorrow is present in every life, and Our Lady shows us that in order to rise with Christ, we must first endure the Cross; the journey to holiness must include sorrow. And when the grief and fear seem too great to bear, Our Lady waits, prays, and weeps with us, consoles us, and ultimately teaches us to persevere in hope. We find solace beneath her mantle—because of her solidarity with our sorrow but even more because of her Immaculate Heart's ability to see past it. Her sorrow is unselfish and grounded in love, and we find consolation there because her ultimate longing is for our hearts—for all of us to be united to her son. Until that time, we weep in sorrowful love for all of mankind, and beg the intercessory prayers of the Theotokos; Our Lady, Undoer of Knots; the Help of Christians. The Mother.

A Rosary for Priests

Sonja Corbitt

This chaplet is a powerful intercessory tool for those who desire to pray for priests and bishops—whether for the repentance of those whose sinful behavior is causing scandal and division, or for the protection and strength of those fighting valiantly against the enemy to defend Christ's Bride, the Church. It can be offered on ordinary rosary beads at any time, but is especially recommended during adoration.

Priests act *in persona Christi* here on earth. Surely it will please the Blessed Mother when we use our rosaries in this special way to intercede for them.

Chaplet of Reparation

Opening prayer:

Incline unto my aid, O Lord, make haste to help me. Glory be to the Father, and to the Son, and to the Holy Spirit, as it was in the beginning, is now, and ever shall be, world without end. Amen.

On the Our Father (large) beads: Eternal Father, I offer You the Most Precious Blood of Your Beloved Son, our Lord Jesus Christ, the Lamb without blemish or spot, in reparation for my sins and the sins of all Your priests.

On the Hail Mary (small) beads: By Your Precious Blood, O Jesus, purify and sanctify Your priests.

In place of the Glory Be: O Father, from whom all fatherhood in heaven and on earth is named, have mercy on all Your priests, and wash them in the Blood of the Lamb. Amen.[6]

This chaplet is from the beautiful book *In Sinu Jesu: When Heart Speaks to Heart*, a journal kept by a Benedictine monk called to a life of adoration and reparation for priests. As a convert to Catholicism from denominationalism, I revel in common devotions, meditations, and prayers that we offer for one another, because often these devotions are backed with the formal power and authority of the ancient Church.

And yet, even the spontaneous, casual prayers of faithful Catholics who join their intentions with those of other faithful believers are guaranteed to have their own power and effectiveness. We know this because of the words of Christ himself: "If two of you agree on earth about anything they ask, it will be done for them by my Father in heaven" (Mt 18:19).

Such is the case with the Chaplet of Reparation. Our priests need us as much as we need them. Though we are rightfully dismayed by the scandals of predation and carnality within the hierarchy of Church leadership, the Holy Spirit is calling us in a new way to sacrifice and pray beautiful prayers such as this one, in reparation for her priests. We seek to cover them in protection and mercy with our prayers and sacrifices, and draw the purifying love of the Holy Spirit down on them in holiness, renewal, and reinvigoration. Let us lift up our beloved priests through prayer to Jesus, knowing it is a privilege of eternal consequence to do so.

Remembering the Joys of Mary

Barb Szyszkiewicz

If you have a particular devotion to St. Francis or St. Clare, the Franciscan Crown is a special way to commemorate their feast days (October 4 and August 11) or to pray anytime. The Franciscan Crown also reminds mothers to look to Mary as our model, our guide, and our friend. You can use a five-decade rosary and double back a bit to complete the seven decades, or purchase a Franciscan Crown rosary.

This devotion commemorates the Seven Joys of Mary:

1. The Annunciation
2. The Visitation
3. The Nativity (Birth) of Our Lord Jesus Christ
4. The Adoration of the Magi
5. The Finding of Jesus in the Temple
6. The Resurrection
7. The Assumption of Mary and Her Coronation as Queen of Heaven and Earth

The Franciscan Crown

Begin with the first Joy of Mary. While reflecting on the Annunciation, pray one Our Father, ten Hail Marys, and one Glory Be (as in the traditional Rosary). After completing the remaining joys in the same manner, pray two more Hail Marys, then one Our Father, Hail Mary, and Glory Be for the intentions of the Holy Father.

I was never taught to pray the Rosary as a child, though both my grandmothers prayed it faithfully, and glow-in-the-dark rosary beads hung on my bedpost. The Franciscan Crown is actually the first Rosary I ever learned to pray (this devotion is not reserved for Franciscans only!).

It's fitting that I learned to pray the Franciscan Crown after I became a mother, because all of the Seven Joys pertain to Mary's motherhood: the first six relate to her as Mother of God, and the last relates to her as mother of us all—and of the Church.

Mothers know that, most of the time, our joys are a bit complicated. Usually they are tinged with sorrow: As our toddler learns to walk, our kindergartner steps confidently into school on the first day, our new driver zips out of the driveway without even waving (and heads, way too fast, toward unknown destinations), we grieve a little, or a lot, for the change that has taken place—even when that change is in itself a good thing.

Mary, our mother, knows that mixture of grief and joy better than any of us. She pondered her joys within her heart, and her sorrows as well. As we ponder the joys of our own motherhood, joys that come with their own challenges and sometimes even sorrows, we can be sure that Mary understands our motherly emotions and concerns. We are not alone in our struggles; we are not alone in our joys.

Walking Step-by-Step with Mary
Susan Wallace

"Hail Mary, full of grace . . ." and already my mind is wandering—racing, actually. My type-A personality finds it hard to slow down. Add a layer of stress, and I can end up absolutely sprinting through a Rosary. Not very soothing. Certainly not listening for God's voice. Not what I had intended when I sat down to pray.

Then, one day, my mother gave me a little blue-and-white book titled *The Scriptural Rosary*. She herself had received it as a gift, and I think she recognized that it was time to hand it on to me. I didn't realize it at the time, but I imagine my stress and suffering were very apparent to my mother. She passed away a short time after, so I was never able to ask her if she found it soothing. She, too, was that type-A, can't-slow-down kind of woman.

Up to that point, I had only randomly prayed the Rosary and must admit I didn't love it. However, as I faced some significant challenges as a young mother, I began to see Mary in a new light. She was no longer just a figure in the Bible. She was a woman, a guide, a mother.

It was through praying the scriptural Rosary that I walked step-by-step, bead-by-bead with Mary and came to see her as a friend and model of the faith. It took a very slow, scriptural Rosary to settle me down enough to hear God's voice and soothe my heart. It helped me let go and give myself to God in a new way.

I love the scriptural Rosary so much. Slow, gentle, peaceful—everything I yearn for, everything I need. And it is then I feel the presence of God in a very personal way, as Mary walks with me like a dear friend.

The Scriptural Rosary

The scriptural Rosary is a modern version of the way the Rosary was once prayed throughout Western Europe in the Late Middle Ages. In the shorter version, brief scripture readings accompany each of the mysteries as indicated on the next page.

THE JOYFUL MYSTERIES

- The Annunciation (Lk 1:26–38)
- The Visitation (Lk 1:39–49)
- The Nativity (Lk 2:6–12)
- The Presentation (Lk 2:22–35)
- The Finding in the Temple (Lk 2:41–51)

THE SORROWFUL MYSTERIES

- The Agony in the Garden (Mt 26:36–39)
- The Scourging at the Pillar (Mk 15:1–2)
- The Crowning with Thorns (Mt 27:27–31)
- The Carrying of the Cross (Lk 23:26–32)
- The Crucifixion (Jn 19:25–30)

THE LUMINOUS MYSTERIES

- The Baptism of Jesus (Mt 3:13–17)
- The Wedding Feast at Cana (Jn 2:1–11)
- The Proclamation of the Kingdom (Mk 2:3–11)
- The Transfiguration (Lk 9:28–36)
- The Institution of the Eucharist (Mt 26:26–29)

THE GLORIOUS MYSTERIES

- The Resurrection (Mt 28:1–6)
- The Ascension (Lk 24:50–53)
- The Descent of the Holy Spirit (Acts 2:1–4)
- The Assumption of Mary (Jud 13:18–20, 15:9)
- The Coronation of Mary (Rv 12:1; Sg 6:10)

Part III

Prayers for a More Intimate Marriage

"Love never ends."
1 Corinthians 13:8

On their wedding day, a man and woman stand before God, as well as friends and loved ones, and promise to love each other "for richer or poorer, in sickness and in health, to love and to cherish . . . until death us do part."

At that moment, love is as sweet and easy as ice cream. No screaming kids (unless one of your married friends brought hers along), no insomnia or stretch marks or stomach flu. No one binging on work, alcohol, or Netflix.

But then, not long after you get back from the honeymoon, it starts to happen. The quirks that you used to find endearing start to bug you. The habits you discover only *after* you begin living with someone come to light. Jobs and friends and houses come and go. You start butting heads over everything from when to visit your families to who empties the trash. The starry-eyed, can't-keep-our-hands-off-each-other stage of honeymoon bliss turns into something much more like a cross.

The good news is that you married your best friend. The not-so-good news is that there is no getting away from him (or from the running, screaming hordes) long enough to use the bathroom in peace. Suddenly "as long as you both shall live" sounds like a life sentence. Then it hits you: This is what your marriage prep group meant when they talked about "self-donating love." No hiding. No quitting. No kidding. God has a cross with your name on it . . . and it looks suspiciously like that handsome guy with the twinkly eyes you fell in love with so long ago. The guy you will fall in love with all over again . . . so long as you keep having and holding each other (and your family) all the way to heaven, where Love greater than you could possibly imagine awaits. These prayers will help get you there.[1]

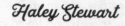

BREATHING GRACE

Haley Stewart

I have trouble sleeping if my husband, Daniel, is out of town. The familiar sound of his breathing as he sleeps beside me is what slows my own breath and beckons me into sleep each night. After fifteen years of marriage, if he is far away it feels as if part of *me* is missing.

"Bone of my bones and flesh of my flesh." This is how scripture describes the intimacy of marriage (Gn 2:23). A parent and a child are bound together by blood, but a husband and wife take on this kind of intimacy by *choice*, reflecting the relationship between God and the Church, his chosen Bride. Through sacramental grace, our spouse—although forever in some ways a mystery to all but God—is made intimately known to us and we to him.

The differences between Daniel and me remain a source of wonder, occasional frustration, and frequent bemusement. "You really like *that*? Your brain works this way?" Even after years of marriage, there are always surprises: from film and food preferences to how we make decisions and communicate. And yet, each day by sacramental grace and as companions through the great sorrows, losses, and also overwhelming joys of life, we are bound together—like comrades in arms through life's battles. We are fellow pilgrims longing for our heavenly home and discovering that it's when we make our soul's dwelling in the heart of God that our hearts are drawn most closely together.

Love's deepest intimacies—whether with Jesus in the tabernacle or your husband next to you—are so often a matter of simple presence. We breathe in the grace, and breathe out our deepest thoughts and feelings to someone who knows us well—and loves us anyway. I wrote the prayer below to celebrate that happiness.

Prayer for a Simple Kind of Love

Heavenly Bridegroom, pour out your grace on my marriage. Guard and protect it, drawing us ever nearer to you, and closer to each other. Nurture the seed of friendship in our hearts that we may take great joy in each other's company. Equip each of us to be more devoted to the good of the other than our own desires. Knit our dreams for life together and make our way forward

76

clear. When we fall short, help us to forgive ourselves; and when our spouse falls short, help us to offer them the same grace to start again without keeping score. Impress upon our hearts that our marriage is more than the love of two people; it is a reflection of your love for the Church. Strengthen us through the grace of the sacraments and prayer to make that reflection beautiful that we may be of one mind, one heart, and one flesh. In the name of the Father, and the Son, and the Holy Spirit. Amen.

BEGGING FOR UNION
Christy Wilkens

In a perfect world, a husband and wife lay down their lives for each other as Christ lays down his body for us in the Eucharist. Both marriage and Holy Communion are sacrament and sacrifice, examples of how dying to self produces life-giving love.

We do not live in a perfect world. Every individual, and every marriage, bears the mark of the Fall in unique and exquisitely painful ways. Stress. Infidelity. Disease. Addiction. Misunderstanding that festers into resentment.

For hope in these dark moments, when love seems lost and our human powers of reconciliation fail, let us draw upon these words: "Never permit me to be separated from You."

That line is from the Spiritual Communion prayer of St. Alphonsus Liguori, a prayer that allows us to commune fully with Jesus in God's mysterious space-time while we are apart in our own. This humble prayer can also unite us with our spouses across emotional distance. Our marriages are each a small reflection of the Sacrament of the Eucharist: a total gift of self, even unto death.

When we are not close, we must beg for union. Turning our thoughts eventually transforms our words and actions. Setting our hearts on communion, rather than our own pain, is the seed that blossoms into renewal. The Sacrament of Marriage bears within itself actual grace, but that grace requires our tenacity, our cooperation, and the lifeblood of Christ.

Return to him. Cling to your promises. Persevere in hope.

Whether the cracks start to show from the outside or the inside, every marriage goes through tough times. Communication becomes strained, with each person going through the motions—yet wanting desperately the happier times ahead. Below is a prayer of hope, that God would use whatever you are facing right now to draw you closer to each other . . . and draw you both closer to him.

Prayer for Healing in Our Marriage

Lord Jesus Christ, Son of God,
Have mercy on our marriage in our time of need.
Thank you for the gift of sacramental, self-giving love.
I am sorry for the ways I have failed to live up to this gift.
Thank you for your strengthening graces when we succeeded.

Lord, my husband and I are distant.
We need communion. We need Communion.
May the gift of yourself in the Eucharist inspire us to love with abandon.
Help us die to ourselves and pour out our lives for each other.

Let the grace of our marriage sacrament enable us
To speak your words,
To listen with your ears,
To understand with your heart,
Align our wills, together and with yours.
Enlighten our hearts and minds with self-knowledge,
and give us your mercy with which to forgive
that which we cannot forgive on our own.

Never permit us to be separated from you.
Never permit us to be separated from each other.
Amen.

OLD WORLD WISDOM

Lyrissa Sheptak

As a newlywed, I found this prayer for wifely humility borderline offensive. I'm a modern woman! I couldn't imagine offering up phrases like "worthy companion," "fulfill my duties," or "please him." Initially I had a strong, negative response to the wording in this prayer: It seemed as if a husband was doing a wife a favor by marrying her, so she'd better make him happy. I had my pride.

Sadly, over time, I learned that was the whole problem. Yes . . . I had my pride. I also learned that this vice doesn't inject intimacy into a relationship. So I took up my Ukrainian Rite prayer book and began to pray for the Old World virtue of humility.

God doesn't intend for us to be slaves to human approval or respect—or to our own woundedness, either. God wants us to live in truth, and as St. Teresa of Avila says, "humility is truth." Humility takes the focus off ourselves and places it on others—just as Christ did for us. Humility leads to grace, and grace helps us achieve holiness. And isn't that what we are called to do—help our spouse attain heaven?

I have learned many lessons since I was a newlywed. Among them, I have learned that humility, sacrifice, duty, and service are not archaic concepts or signs of personal weakness. They are signs of strength and love inspired by Christ himself.

Prayer of Wifely Humility

O Loving and Merciful God, Who in the beginning made Eve out of the side of Adam, to be his companion and helpmate: Give me the grace to be a worthy companion to the man whom You have given me. Help me to love my husband and to comfort him in his troubles. May I please him in everything, for Your sake, and live a pure life until my death.

Keep me from all worldliness and vanity, help me to fulfill my duties as a wife, as a mother, and as the governess of our household. Help me to be a good angel to my husband, to soothe him in perplexity, to cheer him in weariness, to advise him in doubts, and to surround him with Christian love until my death. Grant that we may love You and serve You with one heart and one soul all the days of our life. Amen.[2]

The Road to Safety and Peace

Heidi Hess Saxton

Women in abusive relationships may feel embarrassed or ashamed—whether that abuse is physical, sexual, emotional, or spiritual, the devastation and damage extend not only to you but to your children as well. If for safety's sake you are contemplating separation for yourself and your children, don't be afraid. Make a plan. Ask God to show you the way. If you need help, call the National Domestic Violence Hotline at 800-799-SAFE (7233). If you know a woman in this situation, the best thing you can do is stay connected with her and pray for her. The choice to stay or leave is hers alone.

In *When I Call for Help: A Pastoral Response to Domestic Violence against Women*, the US bishops affirm the right and responsibility of those being abused to protect themselves and their children from harm. These prayers, one of which I adapted from Psalm 55 and the other invoking the intercession of St. Fabiola, the patron saint of abused spouses, are for those who are struggling to find a road to safety and peace.

A Plea for Safety

Give ear to my prayer, O God;
and hide not yourself from my supplication!
Attend to me, and answer me. . . .
My heart is in anguish within me,
the terrors of death have fallen upon me.
Fear and trembling come upon me,
and horror overwhelms me. . . .

It is not an enemy who taunts me—
then I could bear it;
it is not an adversary who deals insolently with me—
then I could hide from him.
But it is you, my equal,
my companion, my familiar friend.

We used to hold sweet converse together;
within God's house we walked in fellowship. . . .

My companion stretched out his hand against his friends,
he violated his covenant.
His speech was smoother than butter,
yet war was in his heart;
his words were softer than oil,
yet they were drawn swords. . . .

But you, O God, will cast them down
into the lowest pit;
men of blood and treachery
shall not live out half their days.
But I will trust in you.
(Psalm 55)

Help Me, St. Fabiola

Dear St. Fabiola, holy and noble, and friend of St. Jerome,
You divorced your first husband for unbearable violence,
And married a second while the first man still lived.
You repented of your error and made lifelong penance,
And the Church blesses you for your courage and costly obedience.
Yet you did not subject yourself or your family to love's counterfeit.

Sweet Fabiola, look down now upon me, and see how I am afraid and
alone.
Pray that I would receive a measure of your courage and wisdom,
And persevere in faith and obedience, no matter how costly.
Protect me and my children under Our Lady's mantle.
Bind my heart to the Love that will never forsake or abuse me.
Open my eyes to the path of righteousness, and close every door of
injustice.

Lord Jesus, have mercy on me, a sinner.
Mary, Queen of Peace, pray for me.
Joseph, Patron of Families, pray for us.
Amen.

When Money Is Tight
Sam (Cecilia) Fatzinger

In more than three decades of marriage, I can't think of a time when money was ever *not* tight! Just when I thought we had our finances straight, the car would break down or we'd get unexpected medical bills. It's one of the ways God keeps us close. Money management is a bit like parenting—you never really get off your knees!

Raising fourteen kids on a single income really makes you walk hand and hand with Christ, and you can't help but see miracles when you least expect them. The best advice I can give when dealing with money is to remind you of my name, SAM: S—Save wherever possible, A—Ask for help (God and others), and M—Make do.

Whenever you are tempted to worry, turn to God and say, "Thy will be done." And when you have a real emergency, offer the Novena to the Infant Jesus of Prague. Honestly, I can say that the Lord has never let our family down!

Some background on this novena: When Prague was invaded in the seventeenth century, a young priest named Fr. Cyril discovered a statue in the ruins of his church. When he picked it up, he heard the infant Jesus say, "The more you honor me, the more I will bless you." Having no money to repair the statue, the priest followed the infant's instructions to place it near the sacristy. The money was miraculously provided, and the statue repaired. Since that time, people have brought their struggles and hopes to the infant King.

This novena consists of a prayer of supplication and a prayer of thanksgiving. You can offer both prayers each day over the course of nine days for a medium-sized emergency, or every hour for nine hours if you *really* need Jesus to take the wheel!

Novena to the Infant Jesus of Prague

Prayer of Supplication

O Jesus, Who has said, "Ask and you shall receive, seek and you shall find, knock and it shall be opened," through the intercession of Mary, Your Most Holy Mother, I knock, I seek, I ask that my prayer be granted. *(Make your request.)*

O Jesus, Who has said, "All that you ask of the Father in My Name, He will grant you," through the intercession of Mary, Your Most Holy Mother, I humbly and urgently ask Your Father in Your name that my prayer will be granted. *(Make your request.)*

O Jesus, Who has said, "Heaven and earth shall pass away but My word shall not pass away," through the intercession of Mary, Your Most Holy Mother, I feel confident that my prayer will be granted. *(Make your request.)*

Prayer of Thanksgiving

Divine Infant Jesus, I know You love me and would never leave me. I thank You for Your close Presence in my life.

Miraculous Infant, I believe in Your promise of peace, blessings, and freedom from want. I place every need and care in Your hands.

Lord Jesus, may I always trust in Your generous mercy and love. I want to honor and praise You, now and forever. Amen.[3]

PORN-PROOF YOUR MARRIAGE

Jackie Francois Angel

Jesus wants us to be free so we may love. But the devil wants to keep us shackled in sin and shame. Shame is a powerful thing. We all know the feeling that St. Paul described in Romans 7:19: "For I do not do the good I want, but the evil I do not want is what I do." Our conscience tells us something is wrong, but our body keeps doing it anyway.

This can describe *all* sin. But because pornography is so widely accessible and has become more culturally acceptable, it's one of the easiest ways for the devil to bring us and keep us under the weight of shame. And the lies that follow continue to pervade one's thoughts: *You're disgusting. No one else does this. You need to hide this. No one will love you. This person/this screen won't reject you. You can stop later; you deserve this,* and on and on.

We must always be on alert to the danger, even with our young children. I heard a friend describe an eight-year-old who had spent a week viewing porn after stumbling across it while on an innocent YouTube search. "I just couldn't stop," he said. That's how porn works: it's like a chemical addiction.

The devil wants us to keep this sin in the dark. To make us feel isolated. To stay trapped under the weight of shame. But Jesus wants to bring the light in. To free us. To heal us. That is why we *must* confess this sin. And we *need* accountability. Only then can we be innocent once again in our hearts, imagination, thoughts, and memories. Only then can we see others as children of God to be loved and not mere objects to be used for pleasure. Only then can we see the goodness of the human body. This freedom and healing will change our lives, our marriages, our children, and future generations. I wrote the following prayer to provide encouragement to stay on that path of freedom and healing.

Prayer for Protection from Pornography

Jesus, by your Precious Blood, protect me and my family from the horrors of pornography. Send your Holy Spirit to renew our innocence, purify our memories and imagination, and enlighten our minds to the truth, beauty, and goodness of the human soul and body created in the image and likeness of God. Help me, my husband, and my children to see the face of God in every person we encounter and to love them as God loves them.

Jesus, I am sorry for the times I have looked upon another as an object for my pleasure, instead of loving them as your son or daughter. Only you, Lord, can heal the shame of pornography in our lives, and we pray for shame to be off of us in the Name of Jesus, so that we may be fully free to love you and our family and our neighbor like the innocent child you have created us to be.

Holy Spirit, make me pure in heart, mind, body, and soul. Mother Mary, cover my family with your mantle to protect us from the demonic influence of pornography and pray for us to be radiant with purity, love, and joy. Amen.

When You Yearn for a Child

Sarah Mackenzie

Are you and your husband longing for a child, or know of someone who is praying for a baby? The St. Andrew Christmas Prayer is a meditation on the Incarnation, traditionally said fifteen times each day beginning November 30, the Feast of St. Andrew, and ending on Christmas Eve.

The first time I prayed this novena was at the urging of a friend who knew my heart ached for a baby. As a convert, I was skeptical; chanting any prayer fifteen times in a row seemed a bit superstitious to me back then. But my heart did long for that baby, so I did it anyway. And, long story short, I got to hold three babies in the next two years; God saw fit to bless us with twins.

The St. Andrew Christmas Prayer is frequently offered by those who desire to conceive, and I have lost count of the babies I know who have been born because of this very prayer. Of course, the hard truth is that the story doesn't always end this way. Even so, the St. Andrew Christmas Prayer taught me something important that had nothing to do with babies. This novena is not about saying a prayer a certain number of times in a certain number of days to "force" God to answer our prayers in the way we hope he will. No, it's about trust. Because when we pray, something shifts. Not in God, perhaps. But certainly in us.

It's about waiting in joyful hope, believing that our prayers do not spiral out into the void. Trusting that they fall into the manger of a tiny holy babe, wrapped in swaddling clothes.

And so we wait. We believe. We trust.

And miracle of miracles—the King of kings is born every year on Christmas day.

The St. Andrew Christmas Prayer

Hail and blessed be the hour and moment in which the Son of God was born of the most pure Virgin Mary, at midnight, in Bethlehem, in the piercing cold. In that hour, vouchsafe, I beseech Thee, O my God, to hear my prayer *(state your intention)* and grant my desires, through the merits of Our Savior Jesus Christ, and of His Blessed Mother. Amen.

PART IV

PRAYERS OF A MOTHER'S HEART

"Whoever receives one such child
in my name receives me."
Mark 9:37

There are as many kinds of mothers as there are children: "artistic moms," who foster their kids' creativity; "granola moms," who focus on good nutrition and healthy habits; even "executive moms," whose type-A personalities are a living embodiment of efficiency, organization, and determination. Much to my kids' chagrin, I'm a bit of a "warrior mom," a bossy fighter and advocator for kids with sad early histories and invisible special needs—but who doesn't always remember to put the shield and sword away when what they need most is a cuddle. I've been working on that . . . and one of these days the gift of gentleness will kick in, and I'll make a great grandmother!

Whatever kind of mom you are and whatever the temperament of your children, your task is the same: to love them here on earth, and all the way to heaven. When my children were little, shortly after their angel (in the form of a beleaguered social worker) brought them to my doorstep, I taught them that God sends every baby into the world with a gift to share, a burden to carry, and a job to do—a job entrusted just to us, because our gifts and burdens have prepared us in a special way.

The prayers in this section are intended to help you build a "triangle of love" between parents, children, and God. Remember, "And though a man might prevail against one who is alone, two will withstand him. A threefold cord is not quickly broken" (Eccl 4:12).

Blessing Prayers for Labor and Delivery

Annabelle Moseley

Each time I was expecting, as my time drew near, my grandmother would remind me of what her brother, a priest, told her right before each of her six labors: "No one is closer to God than a woman in labor." My grandmother lived to the age of 101, and even in her last days, she still loved to recall her brother and spiritual adviser strengthening her with this reminder.

Fr. Tom was a young Jesuit scholastic doing missionary work in the Philippines when World War II struck and the Japanese invaded. He was imprisoned in a war camp and left to starve. When he finally returned to America after the war, malnourished and suffering from malaria, he found my grandmother close to her delivery date. "Please pray for me while you're in labor," he humbly asked, "that God will strengthen me."

From that point on, my grandmother always brought special intentions with her when she went into labor, and she taught me to do the same. Praying for others during labor is a wonderful way to focus one's breathing and keep one's soul centered and aware of the sacredness of the moment. Offer up any pain you experience for your special intentions. I have also found with each of my labors that I have never felt closer to the Communion of Saints.

These two prayers are especially suitable for expectant parents. The Prayer of Humble Trust, taken from Psalm 131, will help a mother focus as she delivers her baby. The Prayer of Consecration to the Infant Jesus may be offered by parents or other family members (adoptive parents, godparents, or grandparents) to bless the child from the first moment after delivery, prior to baptism.

Prayer of Humble Trust

O Lord, my heart is not lifted up;
    my eyes are not raised too high;
I do not occupy myself with things
    too great and too marvelous for me.

But I have calmed and quieted my soul,
    like a child quieted at its mother's breast;
    like a child that is quieted is my soul.
O Israel, hope in the LORD
    from this time forth and for evermore.

Prayer of Consecration to the Infant Jesus

O Infant Jesus, our beloved King,
through the hands of Your loving Mother,
We consecrate *(name)*, our child *(godchild, grandchild)* to You.
Place him/her under Your protection,
save him/her from illness and all harmful influence.
Keep him/her pure
and permit that he/she may grow,
like You, in grace and virtue
before God and men.
Bless *(name)*, Infant Jesus. Amen.[1]

A Marian Lullaby

Derya Little

"The world is thy ship, not thy home," said St. Thérèse of Lisieux, the Little Flower who knew that all things are passing in this world of oblivion, except our love of God and each other. Yet, knowing that this life is only a journey, not the destination, does not always make the choppy waters and dark storms easy to bear.

For me, the long nights of feeding and caring for an infant have numbered among the most trying times of motherhood. Sleeplessness mixed with frustration makes the minutes stretch into hours when the quiet loneliness of the dark becomes oppressive. Despite the hardship, love for my child always pierced through the overcast, making me wake up over and over for months, not because I was strong, but because I found a guiding light in Our Lady.

Whether we are experiencing an unexpected breeze or a threatening storm, Stella Maris guides all of us sailors safely to the harbor of her son. Since I discovered this beautiful prayer composed by St. John Paul II in addition to the version that dates back to the ninth century, petitions to Our Lady, Star of the Sea, escape from my mouth often with the hope that she will give me my footing in the stormy seas of life.

In the gloom of the night, when time slows down, whisper this prayer to Stella Maris for her to subdue the seas and guide you so that you and your little one find peace in this journey of life.

Our Lady, Star of the Sea

O Mary, Star of the Sea,
light of every ocean,
guide us across all dark and stormy seas
that we may reach the haven of peace and light
prepared in him who calmed the sea. . . .

As we set forth upon the oceans of the world
and cross the deserts of our time, show us,
O Mary, the fruit of your womb,
for without your Son we are lost.

Pray that we will never fail on life's journey,
that in heart and mind, in word and deed,
in days of turmoil and in days of calm,
we will always look to Christ and say,
"Who is this that even wind and sea obey him?". . .

O Help of Christians, protect us!
Bright Star of the Sea, guide us!
Our Lady of Peace, pray for us![2]

A MOTHER'S BEDTIME PRAYER

Carrie Schuchts Daunt

With over a decade of experience in healing prayer ministry, I have witnessed many lives transformed in an encounter with God's merciful love. I have watched gaping wounds of the past healed and hardened faces become soft before my eyes.

At the same time, I have held the hands of some who are walking deep into their darkest pain. Listening to their stories, I recognize that most of their experiences are not that different from my own. We are all wounded. And we all wound others. Even our own children. While most of these wounds are inflicted unintentionally, children are most susceptible to the pain a parent causes. These wounds occur not only through what we *do* but also through what we *fail to do* in our vocation as mothers.

With this in mind, I purposefully pray for protection over my children at the end of each day. My prayer is simple and short but serves the purpose of placing each child in the security of Jesus, Mary, and their guardian angel, along with invoking specific coverage over the wounds (the holes) I left exposed that day.

Lord, Fix My Mistakes

Lord Jesus, please bless _____ *(child's name)*.
Cover my child with your Precious Blood.
Fill any holes I have left uncovered.
Mary, wrap my child in your mantle of protection.
Holy Angels, watch over my child as she sleeps.

BLESSED IMPERFECTION

Kelly Johnson

Gratitude for my family is my story.

My mother died young, and unexpectedly. At the funeral, some-one commented that I would always remember her as young and beautiful, which is true—but there isn't a day that goes by that I would not like her here, aging gracefully.

In the years immediately following, we girls (I have four sisters) pulled around my Dad to support and strengthen him, although in fairness, he did the same for us. It bonded us as a family in a way that little us could.

So, when my five-year-old son was diagnosed with a brain tumor, our families and friends demonstrated God's love in action—through meals and visits and just being there, letting us know they were sharing our heartache and pain, worry and prayers. They carried us through a time when we could not carry ourselves, lifting us when we could not.

Each of us needs family. We need community. Our hearts yearn for it. We are birthed from the love of the Trinity into a family. At its best, family is sacred, a reflection of the love God has for all his children. When it is not at its best, the craving does not go away but drives us to find it, to create it. The prayer below comes out of a place of deep gratitude for the family God gave me.

Thank You, Lord, for Family

To you, O Lord, I turn. In your infinite wisdom you gifted me with, and into, my family. It is in this family that you draw me closer to you, Lord.

We are not perfect. But, in those blessed imperfections, you nurture and develop our unique personalities and talents. In the give-and-take of family life, you teach us patience and kindness. In conflict and reconciliation, you show us how to see the other side of a situation. In struggle and difficulty, you remind us to honor the gifts and talents of one another.

Help us, Lord. Heal our disputes and root out our querulous selfishness. Enfold us in your love when we cannot get along. Help me to lead with kind-ness, to be quick to say, "I'm sorry." Remove the past hurts, let them fall away. Help us to speak words to each other that reflect your love and kindness, even when we need to be firm. Help us remember to laugh.

Families are sacred. At the Cross, you did not forsake your family. You gazed with love on your mother and entrusted her care to St. John. So I thank you for the gift of my family. May we be the family you wish us to be, a reflection of your goodness and love. Amen.

THE AVE PRAYER BOOK FOR CATHOLIC MOTHERS

On the First Day of School

Annabelle Moseley

On my eldest son's first day of kindergarten, I watched as he walked away nervously but excitedly, the St. Benedict key chain I had affixed the night before swinging jauntily from his backpack. My son turned around once to look at me, then forged ahead. The pride I felt in his bravery and beauty seared through me. I wondered, *How will he do?*

After he went on his way, I went to daily Mass to light a candle for his first day and pray just for him. The reading for the day was 1 Corinthians 3, in which St. Paul affirmed men he called "infants in Christ." I could feel a burden lifting from my shoulders as I heard these words read: "I planted, Apollos watered, but God gave the growth. So neither he who plants nor he who waters is anything, but only God who gives the growth. He who plants and he who waters are equal, and each shall receive his wages according to his labor. For we are God's fellow workers; you are God's field, God's building" (1 Cor 3:6–9).

I could not get over the grace of this reminder, given on this day of all days—the first day of school. As parents, we plant and water constantly, we watch as our children grow and begin to make their way in the world; but we must remember that it is not us who cause the growth. We are God's laborers, and if our work is sincere, we will be repaid by the Master, but it is "only God who gives the growth."

Prayer to St. Benedict for Blessing and Protection

Dear St. Benedict, monastic saint of peaceful order,
who balanced work and prayer and delight in God,
order our home life that we may balance our portion
of work and worship, perseverance and joy in the Lord.
Strong saint of protection, whose blessed medal keeps demons at bay,
we entrust our family to your guarding and guiding care.
O patron saint of schoolchildren, bless and protect
especially our children. Grant them intelligence in their studies,
diligence in prayer, fortitude in times of challenge, and
deep, abiding love of God. Amen.

Nourishing a Child's Soul

Clare Kilbane

When I was expecting my daughter, I became personally aware of the deep and vital connection between mother and child. Before the end of my first trimester, I realized that everything I consumed, all that I ate or drank, was immediately and intimately transmitted to her. During these months, I grew in inches and pounds—but I also grew in patient trust and a recognition of my lifelong, motherly duty to nourish my child. Over the years, I've learned she needs more than dietary nutrition to grow optimally; she needs spiritual nourishment as well.

Though we are very different people, my daughter and I have a lot in common. We both love dogs and books. We dislike waiting and feeling out of control. There is a blessing in these similarities as they remind us of God's profound gift of our intimate connection. But they also offer a parenting advantage—the personality traits we share make it easier to know when and how my daughter will need special spiritual support.

When I first encountered this prayer of patient trust by Fr. Teilhard de Chardin during my pregnancy, it resonated deeply with me. I've returned to it again and again for consolation and inspiration. As my daughter approaches adulthood, and grows to be very much like her mother, I look forward to sharing it with her so that it can nourish her spiritual life as it has mine.

Patient Trust

Above all, trust in the slow work of God.
We are quite naturally impatient in everything to reach the end
without delay.
We should like to skip the intermediate stages.
We are impatient of being on the way to something unknown,
something new.

And yet it is the law of all progress
that it is made by passing through some stages of instability—
and that it may take a very long time.

And so I think it is with you;
your ideas mature gradually—let them grow,
let them shape themselves, without undue haste.
Don't try to force them on,
as though you could be today what time
(that is to say, grace and circumstances acting on your own good will)
will make of you tomorrow.

Only God could say what this new spirit
gradually forming within you will be.
Give Our Lord the benefit of believing
that his hand is leading you,
and accept the anxiety of feeling yourself
in suspense and incomplete.[3]

Unlocking the Mysteries of My Child

Christine Kelly Baglow

No matter how many joys and blessings we may count, motherhood still comes with challenges. Today, more than ever before, many mothers spend their lives caring and advocating for children who struggle with challenges invisible to the untrained eye. We are the mothers of children with neurodiverse diagnoses such as ASD, APD, SPD, ADHD, ADD, OCD, ODD, and so on.

The words below of Elizabeth Ann Foss, from her book *Real Learning Revisited*, have become an often-repeated prayer of mine as I parent my children. The mystery inherent in these questions casts a deeper shadow with my special-needs children than with my neurotypical ones. But this shadowland is also an immeasurable blessing. I must observe more intentionally, advocate more heroically, and ask for graces with more humility, knowing that I am incapable of doing this all on my own.

Jesus is with me as I ponder the complexity of their lives and strive to educate, form, catechize, socialize, dress, and feed children whose abilities in many areas of life are . . . *different*. I gaze in wonder at how God is fashioning them, and am reminded that we ought to always stand in awe of one another, because we are each uniquely made in God's image and likeness.

Children with special needs are equal sharers in the Divine Image, in the life of grace, and are full members of the Body of Christ. Sometimes we run short on energy, love, and patience. Maybe we neglect prayer because we're just too doggone tired, overwhelmed, or discouraged. But our loving and merciful Lord takes our meager offerings and transforms them into an ocean of grace for ourselves and our kids. As we can learn from this brief reflection, God renews us abundantly if we but turn to him, ask for his help, and listen.

A Parent's Reflection on a Child with Special Needs

Who is this child?
For what have You created him?
How can I equip him to answer Your call?[4]

Letting God Take Over

Eileen Zimak

Motherhood is a great gift, but it can also be a bit confusing. For nine months, we carry our children in our bodies. Once they make their grand appearance, we feed them, bathe them, clothe them, and tend to their every need. As time goes by, we may not do as much, but we are still very much in charge of their lives. "Eat this. Don't eat that. Wear this. Don't forget your hat. Do your homework. Go to bed. Wake up." You get the idea! As mothers, we get very used to calling the shots. Even though we complain about it sometimes, deep down it feels good to be in control.

In the blink of an eye, however, things change. They don't seem to need us like they used to. Suddenly, words like "driver's permit," "dating," and "college" present themselves in everyday conversations. Wait. What? The realization hits us like a ton of bricks. It's time to loosen our grip and start letting go. Not an easy task—almost impossible, you might say. Panic can settle in when we realize we're no longer in control. What will become of them? What will their future look like?

I have found great comfort in this Bible verse, found in the book of Jeremiah: "For I know the plans I have for you, says the LORD, plans for welfare and not for evil, to give you a future and a hope" (29:11).

I may not know my children's future, but God does. When the time comes, it's okay to let go, because they never leave *his* sight.

Prayer for Letting Go

Dear Lord, my child is getting older.
They don't seem to need me as much as they used to.
It's tough for me to loosen my grip.
Help me to let go and to let you take over.
Help me to remember that you love my child even more than I do
and that you have great things in store for them.
Amen.

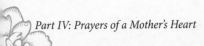

WHEN CHOICES HAVE CONSEQUENCES
Rose Sweet

"Officer, his father and I have discussed this, and we agree: he should stay the night in jail to learn a lesson."

It was three a.m. and I had shuffled out of bed to the phone while my husband was still snoring. One of my three, smart, perfect, teen-aged stepsons had been arrested for being a bystander when an infamous teen tagger—a local legend, really—had finally been caught in the act. I figured we could get him in the morning and later decide the consequences of his following the wrong crowd.

"I don't think you understand, ma'am." The officer paused. "This is San Francisco City Jail. With the rough criminals we have here, your son may not be safe through the night."

Gulp! I woke my husband and off we went.

That was years ago, and I laugh about it now, thanking God I had five brothers growing up. The truth is that I fell in love with each of my stepsons when I married their dad. We have no biological bonds, but the heartstrings of caring, teaching, guiding, disciplining, laughing, and loving have tied me tightly to them forever.

I love them fiercely and would fight ferociously for them. I still climb out of bed and go to my knees for them every morning. My prayer is short, to the point, and covers all that I want most for them: to first seek and follow the Lord with all their heart. No one and nothing else.

A Prayer of Hope for My Sons

Gracious Father, grant our boys
Wisdom to first seek only you,
Work that makes them strong and true,
Women of virtue to be their spouses, and a
Wealth of children to fill their houses.
Amen.

Patient Parenting

Lauren Nelson

"Lord, put your arm around my shoulder and your hand over my mouth."

I find myself repeating this prayer often as the mother of two daughters; it is my own version of Psalm 141:3. Sometimes I say it before my feet even hit the floor in the morning. I am not a patient person, but as I adjust the seam on my seven-year-old's sock for the seventh time that morning, I pray for God to show me how to be a kind and caring parent. I am also not a morning person, but as my ten-year-old talks and talks, I pray for the grace to be a good listener and offer a smile.

I frequently need the guidance and reassurance of God's gentle presence to help me with the decisions that come with mothering daughters. Big decisions like, "What do I say when they ask the tough life questions?" as well as the seemingly little decisions like, "Pink bow or red scrunchie?" (Either choice will inevitably cause a fight.)

This is where the final part of the prayer comes into play. I often need God to put his hand over my mouth *before* I cause more conflict with my daughters. There are times I want to tell my daughters what to choose, but this prayer reminds me to ask for the wisdom to let them decide, to keep my mouth shut, and to guide them in the right direction with as much gentleness as my heavenly Father has always guided me.

A Prayer for Parents with Daughters

I call upon you, O Lord; make haste to me!
> Give ear to my voice, when I call to you!
Let my prayer be counted as incense before
> you,
>> and the lifting up of my hands as an
>> evening sacrifice!
Set a guard over my mouth, O Lord,
> keep watch over the door of my lips!
(Psalm 141:1–3)

MODELING GOODNESS

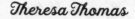

Theresa Thomas

I am so grateful to the friend who introduced me to the *Mother Love* prayer book, which contains this prayer about modeling virtue for our children. It is such a beautiful, earnest, and sincere plea to God to help us know our responsibility in raising our children, and to help us fulfill that responsibility.

Most moms carefully choose healthy and nutritious food for their babies' growing bodies, but this prayer reminds us that what we put into our children's hearts and minds (how to know, love, and serve God), or allow in the home (such as movies, books, music, and attitudes), must also be wholesome and "organic." We are what we eat, the old adage goes, and this prayer reminds us that taking in only good things is critical to not only physical but spiritual growth. This prayer also reminds us that we are examples, and that children watch what we do and emulate us. We must model the behavior and attitude that we wish our children to have.

There are so many dangers and temptations in this world. My daily prayer for every one of my children is simple: "Dear Lord, protect them in mind, body, and soul." The prayer below details this request and desire. I love how the prayer commends our children to God. He loves them even more than we do. He's got them covered!

Prayer for Lifelong Virtue

O good God, we thank Thee, that Thou hast given us children, made them heirs of heaven by holy baptism and entrusted to us their training. Penetrate us with a sense of our responsibility; assist us in the care of their health, but especially in the preservation of their innocence and purity of heart. Grant that we may teach them early to know and serve Thee, and to love Thee, with their whole heart. Grant that we ourselves may carefully avoid all that we must forbid them, and may assiduously practice all that we should teach them. We commend them, O God, to Thy paternal care and to the guardianship of Thy holy angels. Bless our efforts, O heavenly Father, and let our children develop to Thy honor and persevere in virtue till the end! Amen.[5]

When I Feel Overwhelmed

Elizabeth Sri

The huge learning curve of new motherhood drove home one simple fact—I had no idea what I was doing. I felt completely overwhelmed in everything related to my vocation as wife and mom. As the number of children, diapers, and demands in life grew, my energy levels plummeted. I was swallowed alive by unfolded laundry, untouched library books, and unfulfilled life goals.

When I felt like I was drowning, this prayer became a sturdy lifeline. Through it I ask Jesus, just for today, to step in and fix the things I've screwed up, both the glaring mistakes I see in my home and the ones I've yet to discover. Jesus, fill in the gaps for all the unchecked to-do items, the list that seems to grow by the hour. Repair the bad, Lord, and supply for my many "undones."

Twenty years in, this simple uttering of the heart developed a deeper meaning. The staggered exodus of grown children from our home has begun, off to college and beyond. I know I've not been the perfect mother. I know I've not done all I could. Yet I am at peace. Jesus did repair and supply. And I trust he will continue to do so . . . for they truly are more his children than mine after all.

The Little Way for Imperfect Moms

Jesus, repair what I have done badly,
supply for what I have left undone.[6]

The Gift of My Husband's Daughter

Sherry Hayes-Peirce

When I met my husband fifteen years ago, he told me, "If my daughter doesn't like you, it's over." Some women might have been angered by that, but to me it spoke volumes about this man's character and integrity. Thankfully, Brianna liked me!

Over the course of many years I have watched her graduate from middle school, high school, and college; settle into a career and get married; and now become a mother of two. She is strong, smart, and independent. I always hated the term "step," so I have always referred to Brianna as my "gifted daughter," because she is a gift to me. Yet we have shared some difficult times that prompted me to write the prayer below.

Do you have a "gifted" child in your life? Why not memorize this little prayer or keep it close, so that when crises arise in your relationship, you will be ready to ask the Blessed Mother for help!

A Stepmother's Prayer

Mother Mary, model of motherhood,
Help me to love this "gifted" child, my husband's daughter.
Open my ears to listen to the message you want to send me
in this difficult time.
Shield my heart from hurtful words and impulsive acts.
Help me to recognize that what was said and done
comes from their own pain.
Train my tongue to speak words of encouragement,
Give me a heart that seeks to heal the enmity between us.
Guide me in how to be the stepmom that she needs me to be.
Close my mind to any thoughts of jealousy or judgment.
Inspire me to love her, even when she doesn't love me back.
Help her love me and want to be
A little bit like me.
Amen.

THE POWER OF PRAYER

Mary Amore

We live in precarious times. Online and in real life, our grandchildren witness tragic events, civil unrest, world catastrophes, and even attacks against the faith that were once unimaginable, affecting youthful innocence and distorting their focus. It is hard not to lose hope when we think of the world we are handing on to them. So what is a Christian grandmother to do?

One of the most life-giving legacies we can offer our grandchildren is to pray for them every single day. We may not be physically present to guide them in their daily lives, but never underestimate the power of prayer. God is with them, and they are never alone. Believing this takes a deep and unshakable faith in God. Each day, bless your grandchildren as they go out into the world, knowing that the Lord is with them, and that he loves them more than we could ever imagine.

A Grandmother's Prayer

Lord God,
You are the giver of all that is good.
Thank you for blessing me with my family,
most especially my grandchildren.
They are the fulfillment of my life.
I lovingly entrust my grandchildren to your care.
Keep them safe in these uncertain times.
Protect them from the forces of this world
that seek to cause them bodily, spiritual, or mental harm.
Give them your Spirit of wisdom
to lead and guide their actions each day.
If they falter and stray from your path,
welcome them with your abundant mercy and compassion
when they return home.
Instill in them reverence and respect for all that you have created.
I place them in your care.
In Jesus' name, I pray. Amen.

CREATED OUT OF SHEER LOVE

Mallory Smyth

The more I fall in love with God, the more I fall in love with birthdays. Behind the cake, the presents, and the chaos, there is a mystery waiting to be explored. That mystery is the glory of God that is reflected in our existence.

The first sentence of the *Catechism of the Catholic Church* reveals this mystery in beautiful language: "God, infinitely perfect and blessed in himself, in a plan of sheer goodness freely created man to make him share in his own blessed life" (*CCC* 1).

Did you catch that? God did not create us out of need; he is perfectly blessed and complete within himself. So why then did he create us, especially if he knew that we would mess everything up? He created us because he is love and love creates. When God set each person's existence in motion, he revealed not only his love, but his utter extravagance. He has an unrelenting desire to fill the world with his goodness.

You and your child are a sign of God's over-the-top desire to adorn the world with his beauty. With this in mind, consider this little paragraph that I often add to my birthday cards. "Did you know that God did not need you? God is perfect and needs nothing. Instead, God looked over the world and asked himself, 'How can I add to its delight?' And then, out of love, he crafted you. You were not needed but wanted, desired from the beginning, and your very existence is a fresh breath of God's life to this world."

A Birthday Prayer

Eternal Father, you are the creator and giver of all life. Thank you for creating *(child's name)* out of sheer love, to share in your life and to bring your goodness into the world. You know exactly who you created him to be. You know for exactly what purpose he exists.

Today, on his birthday, I offer *(name)* back to you, this precious gift that you have entrusted to me. I ask you to foster the truth of his identity as your child in his own heart, so that when he looks in the mirror, he sees that you delight in him. Protect him from the lies and actions of the enemy,

and guard him from those in the world that would derail him from fulfilling your purpose for his life.

Lord, please give me the understanding and wisdom I need to foster his unique personality and gifts. Bless him and infuse him with the power and presence of the Holy Spirit. Thank you for making him part of our family—someone who is so creative and funny, who we love and delight in. Help us to help him grow into the person you created him to be. Amen.

PART V

PRAYERS FOR HELP IN TIMES OF TRIAL

"Count it all joy."
James 1:2

"Count it all joy, my brethren," wrote the apostle James, "when you meet various trials, for you know that the testing of your faith produces steadfastness. And let steadfastness have its full effect, that you may be perfect and complete, lacking in nothing" (Jas 1:2–4).

Although he was writing to his "brethren," I have to believe James was *thinking* of their wives. As mothers, we generally live closest to the ground in times of crisis, managing the day-to-day details: the meal trains, doctor appointments, and teacher conferences. And because as women we are inherently relational, it also falls to us to track the prayer intentions of those we care about—when a familiar name turns up in the Prayers of the Faithful, parish prayer chain, or a Facebook posting, we take it to heart. Then we take it to God.

The prayers in this section are intended to enrich the arsenal of favorite prayers you already keep at the ready. They appear alongside short reflections of mothers like you who have persevered in faith and pushed through to grace. May their examples and their offerings encourage you to "count it all joy"—even when the temptation to worry about the future is strong.

STAY WITH ME, LORD

Jenna Guizar

The story of the walk to Emmaus is one of my favorite gospel passages. I'm happy to hear that it must have been one of St. John Paul II's favorites as well:

> "Stay with us, Lord, for it is almost evening" (Lk 24:29). . . . Amid the shadows of the passing day and the darkness that clouded their spirit, the Wayfarer brought a ray of light which rekindled their hope and led their hearts to yearn for the fullness of light. "Stay with us," they pleaded. And he agreed. Soon afterwards, Jesus' face would disappear, yet the Master would "stay" with them, hidden in the "breaking of the bread" which had opened their eyes to recognize him.[1]

The idea of the Lord walking with us, step-by-step, on this Christian journey is an image I come back to nearly daily in my prayer. The truth that I am not alone on the way, no matter how alone I may feel—in my marriage, as a mother, as a friend, as a daughter—has changed my life.

No matter how discouraging my day can be—from the endless piles of dishes and laundry and toys and chores to the distance I feel from my husband when we are experiencing desolation in our relationship—I have a companion, a Savior, a friend who never leaves my side.

There are times, of course, when I choose to stray: times I lose my temper with my children; times I choose to overindulge in shopping, drinking, or Netflix; times I shut my husband out because *how will he ever understand?* Every day, every hour, every moment we can choose either to continue walking alongside the Lord on the way to our eternal home, or to turn from him and carve our own path, make our own choices, move in alignment with our own will.

But Jesus never leaves. He stays, waiting for us to turn our gaze back to him and invite him to stay with us. He will always draw close, come into the home of our hearts, and set them on fire with his love, presence, and Spirit.

In every moment, in all temptation, irritation, discouragement, or fear, let us always remember to turn our gaze to our Savior who is always present, and ask, "Stay with me, Lord." And he always will.

I put together this litany for any time you want to be more mindful of the Holy Spirit's movements in your life throughout the day. Whether you are feeling anxious or lonely, or simply find yourself trying to cope with an overwhelming task, this litany extends a simple invitation of encounter with the one who loves us best.

The response (R) for this litany is, *Stay with me, Lord.*

A Litany of Trust

Stay with me, Lord Jesus.

In the joyful noisiness of this day—R

In suffering and sickness—R

In dying and rising—R

In detachment from the world—R

In turning away from sin—R

In the quest for virtue—R

In the interior quiet of my heart—R

In intercession and contemplation—R

In communion with you—R

Walk with me, step-by-step,

As I make a gift of myself—R

In tasks great and small—R

In uncomfortable conversations—R

In laughter and friendship—R

In tending to family—R

Let me feel you close by

As I step out in courage—R

In tears and in sorrow—R

In every disappointment—R

In moments of fear—R

In lingering hope—R

Open my eyes to see you before me
   In the breaking of the bread—R
   In your eucharistic presence—R
   In my burning heart—R

Walk with me, step-by-step, on the road ahead—R

Battling the Enemy

Marge Steinhage Fenelon

I was introduced to the Chaplet of St. Michael the Archangel by a friend who had recommended it to me not knowing that our family was embroiled in spiritual combat, and had been for years. Things had gotten increasingly difficult as time passed, and when the most pronounced attack occurred, I believe God prompted my friend to call in order to show me that we were not alone in our battle—that the angels themselves were fighting on our behalf. As I read the chaplet for the first time, it was so beautiful that I immediately fell in love with it.

The nine choirs, or levels, of angels and their works are infused in scripture: seraphim (Is 6:2–6) and cherubim (Gn 3:24; Is 37:16), thrones and dominions (Col 1:16), virtues and powers (Eph 1:21; 1 Pt 3:22, D-R), archangels (Jude 1:9), principalities (Rom 8:38), and of course . . . angels, including guardian angels (Ps 91:11). The St. Michael Chaplet, then, is an intercessory tool that calls on the warriors of heaven to defend God's children from evil on the earth.

When my husband and I sought the guidance of a priest specially trained in exorcism and spiritual warfare, Father confirmed that we were under a brutal attack of the evil one and suggested—you guessed it—the Chaplet of St. Michael along with other things we could do to thwart these demonic attacks. It worked!

I now pray the Chaplet of St. Michael daily. It gives me peace, strength, and consolation knowing that St. Michael and the nine choirs of angels are protecting and interceding for my family and anyone else for whom I pray.

St. Michael himself gave this chaplet to a Portuguese Carmelite nun named Antonia d'Astonac in a private revelation in 1751. A century later, it was approved by Pope Pius IX. Below are the concluding prayers of the chaplet, which are a beautiful reminder of how the angels defend and protect us in the fight against evil.

Chaplet of St. Michael the Archangel

(Concluding Prayers)

O glorious prince St. Michael, chief and commander of the heavenly hosts, guardian of souls, vanquisher of rebel spirits, servant in the house of the Divine King and our admirable conductor, you who shine with excellence and superhuman virtue deliver us from all evil, who turn to you with confidence and enable us by your gracious protection to serve God more and more faithfully every day.

Pray for us, O glorious St. Michael, Prince of the Church of Jesus Christ, that we may be made worthy of His promises.

Almighty and Everlasting God, Who, by a prodigy of goodness and a merciful desire for the salvation of all men, has appointed the most glorious Archangel St. Michael Prince of Your Church, make us worthy, we ask You, to be delivered from all our enemies, that none of them may harass us at the hour of death, but that we may be conducted by him into Your Presence. This we ask through the merits of Jesus Christ Our Lord. Amen.[2]

Entrusting a Child to God in a Medical Emergency

Sarah Christmyer

We kissed our newborn one last time as they wheeled him into the operating room. The doors swung shut and I collapsed on a nearby bench. *God!* I cried. *Where are you?* I couldn't wrap my mind around the fact that our son was born with a life-threatening heart defect. I couldn't bear the thought of them cutting into his chest. Would he live? Would we see him again? *O Lord, please be with him!*

I opened my Bible, looking for comfort. These words from Psalm 33 jumped out at me: "The Lord looks down from heaven, he sees all the sons of men . . . he who fashions the hearts of them all. . . ."

God, you made him! My own heart stopped as I considered this truth. Not that God purposefully made a defective heart, but that he created, loves, and sees my son. As I read on and prayed, I was assured that God loves our son more than we do, and that he entrusted our son to our care. Psalm 33 held us steady in hope throughout that difficult time: "Let your mercy, O Lord, be upon us, even as we hope in you."

Whose heart do you need to entrust to the Lord today?

Read the selections below from Psalm 33 slowly and prayerfully. Pause at words or phrases that catch your attention, and let God speak to you through the scriptures.

A Psalm of Surrender

The Lord looks down from heaven,
　　he sees all the sons of men;
from where he sits enthroned he looks forth
　　on all the inhabitants of the earth,
he who fashions the hearts of them all,
and observes all their deeds. . . .

Behold, the eye of the LORD is on those who fear him,
  on those who hope in his merciful love,
that he may deliver their soul from death,
  and keep them alive in famine.
Our soul waits for the LORD;
  he is our help and shield.
Yea, our heart is glad in him,
  because we trust in his holy name.

Let your mercy, O LORD, be upon us,
  even as we hope in you.
(Psalm 33:13–15, 18–22)

Familiar Sins

Bonnie Rodgers

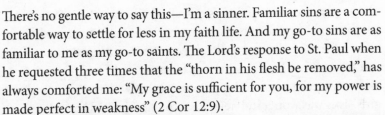

There's no gentle way to say this—I'm a sinner. Familiar sins are a comfortable way to settle for less in my faith life. And my go-to sins are as familiar to me as my go-to saints. The Lord's response to St. Paul when he requested three times that the "thorn in his flesh be removed," has always comforted me: "My grace is sufficient for you, for my power is made perfect in weakness" (2 Cor 12:9).

The Morning Offering given below resonates with me because the prayer truly summarizes to me that each thing I say and do must glorify God and his people. When I stumble into a familiar sin, I have saints that I lean on for wisdom. And when I realize that I am holding on to sins that satisfy my own needs and not the will of God, I add a simple phrase ("my failures and sins") to my morning offering: I offer them up to the Sacred Heart, knowing he will take them from me.

The line "for all the intentions of Your Sacred Heart" reminds me of my connection to the Sacred Heart, and of the School Sisters of Notre Dame who fostered that link through my education at our parish school. They cultivated in me a devotion to the Sacred Heart and a commitment to the spiritual and corporal works of mercy—sort of a schoolgirl version of *ora et labora* and the familiar "offer it up!"

Offering your day to God each morning, whether in your own words or with a favorite prayer like the one below, is a habit that bears rich spiritual fruit. Just as exercise is essential for your physical health, so is a habit of prayer essential for the health of your soul.

My Morning Offering

O Jesus, through the Immaculate Heart of Mary, I offer You my prayers, works, joys, [failures and sins], and sufferings of this day in union with the Holy Sacrifice of the Mass throughout the world. I offer them for all the intentions of Your Sacred Heart: the salvation of souls, reparation for sin, and the reunion of all Christians. I offer them for the intentions of our bishops and of all Apostles of Prayer, and in particular for those recommended by our Holy Father this month.[3]

THERE IS ALWAYS HOPE

Eileen Zimak

The doctor's face was somber as he walked into the office. "I'm sorry to tell you this, but your babies only have a 10 percent chance to be born alive." I felt the walls start to close in on me when I heard those words. Just twenty-four hours earlier, my husband and I had learned at my eighteen-week ultrasound appointment that we were expecting twin girls. This was wonderful news for a couple who had been struggling to get pregnant for three years. How did our world turn upside down so quickly? In a matter of minutes, a sickening sense of hopelessness fell upon us.

After the news sank in and we got over our initial shock, my husband and I knew what we had to do. We put our daughters completely in God's care. We reached out to everyone we knew and asked them to pray. Pray as hard as they could. We forced ourselves to take one day at a time and not to think ahead. Most importantly, we constantly reminded ourselves that God was in control. He was our only hope.

Every evening when we said our Rosary, we were filled with an overwhelming sense of peace. But for ten weeks, we were on a roller-coaster ride. Some days were good, and some days were horrible. The one constant was our firm belief that God had our babies in the palm of his hand, and we resigned ourselves to his holy will.

Maybe you find yourself in a similar situation. If so, here is something I want you to hang onto: There is always hope. At twenty-eight weeks, our beautiful girls were born. Today, they are healthy and happy young women whose very existence shows everyone they meet that miracles happen.

I wrote the prayer below for those moments when you need a little hope and a reminder that, with God, all things are possible.

Prayer during a Troubled Pregnancy

Dear Lord, thank you for the gift of this pregnancy and for the awesome privilege of being able to participate in the creation of new life. But, Lord, I'm scared. My pregnancy is in trouble. The doctors have given me little hope.

Even though this baby grows inside of me, I feel so helpless. I place my child in your hands, confident that you can help. Give me the courage to accept your will. Amen.

AFTER MISCARRIAGE
Stephanie Gray Connors

[W]hen someone is dying, you think that room [they are in] is part of this earth? No! You are not in this world. You have entered the vestibule of heaven.

Dr. Michael Brescia[4]

A second line on a pregnancy test declared I was a first-time momma at age forty. My husband and I received this news with great joy, naming our baby Laetificat Judah ("LaeLae"). The three weeks we were aware of LaeLae's life were glorious. I especially loved introducing LaeLae to Jesus: When I received the Body of Christ at Mass, I imagined my child leaping like John the Baptist at the eucharistic Jesus entering the tabernacle of my body as she nestled nearby in my womb.

But a short while later, my husband and I entered the "vestibule of heaven" as our LaeLae began to leave my body. We prayed the Psalms aloud from the first signs of miscarriage, to send Laetificat Judah to our heavenly home: "You show me the path of life; in your presence there is fulness of joy" (Ps 16:11). "He reached from on high, he took me, he drew me out of many waters" (Ps 18:16).

My husband baptized LaeLae, and we held a funeral and burial. (No matter how young your baby, you can collect the blood for burial.) As part of my grieving process, I have let myself imagine how, one day in the future, I will stand at the gates of heaven and see my Savior holding the hand of a little girl who has thick, curly brown hair and who's wearing a blue dress, and she'll whisper to me, "Welcome home, Mommy."

Until that day, pray for me, St. LaeLae.

Prayer When a Baby Has Died

Heavenly Father, thank you for this precious child, whose very existence made me a mom. As the Book of Job declares that you *give and take away*, I thank you for giving this child; I trust that my little one's taking away is only temporary; and I choose to say *blessed be your name*. I entrust this little soul into your hands and wait with hope for the day when we will be reunited in the world to come, where there are no more tears. Until then, please heal my aching heart and impregnate my mind with peace. Amen.

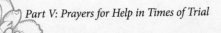

As I Recover from Childbirth

Corynne Staresinic

It is easy for me to look at my pregnancy, labor and postpartum journey as signs of shame or divine punishment — the cost of the blessing of new life. It is easy for me to believe that the suffering accompanying early motherhood isolates me from my Creator. Between the high hospital bills from delivery, a stubborn UTI I got from giving birth, and all of the hormonal shifts that come with the postpartum journey, it is tempting for me to believe that God has indeed turned his back on me.

My fertility—the cause of these events—often feels like a liability, not a privilege. And yet, a line from scripture has been echoing in the back of mind these past three and a half months since my son's birth. I hear it when I breastfeed. I hear it when I look at my baby. I hear it when I look at a crucifix. It is perhaps a whisper of truth about this situation: *This is my body which is given for you* (Lk 22:19).

Inspired by these sacred words, I wrote the prayer below to remind myself that all of these things—the pain of pregnancy, the blood of birth, the rigor of recovery—are signs that Jesus is here, that my body is an image of God, and that even though life has felt chaotic these past few months, there is hope on the horizon.

Help Me to See You: A New Mother's Prayer

God my Creator,
You made me—a woman and mother—
in your image and likeness,
you look upon me and see me as good,
you know the path before me,
a path not for my woe, but toward a future of hope.
In my capacity to create, carry, and birth new life, my dear God,
there you are present, your love for me revealed in my body.
Help me to see you here.

Jesus, my Savior and friend,
you have said to me, "This is my body which is given for you."
You have wept, bled, and died for me,

you have shown me that there is no greater love than this,
than to give up one's life for another.
In my tears,
in the blood shed,
in the marks on my belly,
my dear Jesus, you are present,
your love revealed in this sacrifice.
Help me to see you here.

Holy Spirit, healer and bestower of grace,
you have revealed that I make up what is lacking in Christ's afflictions,
you bestow depth and meaning to any small moment,
It is you who makes all things whole.
In the eyes of my baby,
in these sleepless nights,
in these hormonal shifts,
my dearest Guide, you are present,
working toward hope, making me whole.
Help me to see you here.

FOR THE CHILD I DON'T GET TO KEEP

Marcia Lane-McGee

Crossing a bridge terrifies me. I have an irrational fear that it's going to give out right from under me and I will have to rely on my mediocre swimming prowess to save my life. Of course, this doesn't stop me from crossing when the time comes. I grew up in Chicago, and crossing the river was a fact of life. San Francisco is one of my favorite cities, so I am no stranger to the 1.7 miles from one end of the Golden Gate Bridge to the other. The thing is, I trust these bridges. I know they're strong. I know they are experienced. I know they can take me on.

Every day I try to be like a bridge for my boys. My mom story is a little different from most: I am a birth mom. That means that I had a child I didn't get to keep. I was twenty-three, pregnant, scared, and practically homeless when I made an adoption plan for my son. Though our adoption is open and I get to be a part of his life, my heart will always be broken that he wasn't mine to keep. Loving him and the family I chose for him has opened my heart to continue on a path of loving and letting go.

A lot of life has happened since the moment I placed my child in another woman's arms. I've made other choices and taken other chances, such as running Mooseheart Child City and School, an organization dedicated to serving children at every stage. Among them are teen boys, who are all at once creative, forgetful (especially when it comes to doing chores), sensitive, smelly, challenging . . . and mine. Mine to guard and mine to guide. For now. My boys have families of their own, and they are with me for different reasons. All that is important to know is that they need me in this moment in time and it is my privilege to shield them from the raging waters.

I can take the currents.

No, it is not always easy. I often have to answer for the parent who is not present, bear the brunt of it in the first moments when trust is hard, or redirect the independence that comes from growing up too fast. Those are the moments when I pray, "Lord, let me be a bridge." And I pray for the other bridges they may encounter because in this life there are many rivers to cross.

But now, right now, I am their bridge. They know they can trust me, that I am strong. They may test me at times, but they know I can take them on for as long as I am needed.

I don't get to keep, but I get to care.

I don't get to keep, but I get to cultivate.

Lord, Give Me Strength

Lord, let me be a bridge.
Grant me the strength to blaze a trail
until it becomes a well-worn path.
Let my girders be secure
as loads are dropped to ease the journey.
Give me fortitude to withstand the floods
to allow my travelers safe passage.
And the humility to seek reinforcement
when I no longer feel sufficient. Amen.

FOR FAMILIES IN CRISIS

Anne DeSantis

Through my work at the St. Raymond Nonnatus Foundation for Freedom, Family, and Faith, I've worked with hundreds of families in crisis. The foundation was established by the Order of Mercy (the Mercedarians) as a tangible expression of their fourth vow, to "offer their lives for those in danger of losing their faith."

As the director of this nonprofit, I help families who have suffered loss, divorce, or other crisis. I have seen the power of prayer at work in the lives of families, them to persevere in challenging times with the help and strength of our Lord and the Church. I recommend this prayer for anyone whose family is experiencing a crisis or special challenge. As you pray, may you and your family grow ever closer to Jesus, our Blessed Mother, and the countless angels and saints watching over us.

Lord, Be Our Safe Place Now

Lord Jesus, thank you for the gift of life and of family. Thank you for providing for me and my loved ones right now. I humbly come to you at this moment simply to thank you and to ask for more of your presence in my life.

I trust you, Lord God, and I ask you to help me to trust you more, especially during this time of crisis in my life. My family is going through a very rough time, and I am not sure of the future. Mother Mary, you are our mother, and I come to you with my prayer for peace. Help me to do God's will as my family and I work through our challenges.

Lord, give me guidance, strength, perseverance, and protection during this crisis. Please use this spiritual battle to help my family grow in faith, hope, and love. Lord, I especially ask you to be with my children as they navigate through the sadness and pain they are experiencing. We love and trust you, Lord Jesus Christ. We want to follow you all the days of our life. Help us, as a family, to love you more than ever during this difficult time. Amen.

Praying for My Enemies
Leah Libresco Sargeant

One of the picture books I look forward to reading to my baby daughter is *Sometimes I'm Bombaloo*, by Rachel Vail. In this book, five-year-old Katie is sometimes so carried away by her anger that she doesn't feel like Katie anymore but "Bombaloo," who rampages around the house.

Like Katie, we may find it liberating at first to be unrestrained in our feelings, but sooner or later, anger, like all sins, starts to feel like a prison we've locked ourselves into. Below is the prayer I use to unlock the door and ask for help. I get angry often enough that I keep the prayer saved on my phone.

This prayer meets me in the heat of my anger, when I don't want to pray for my brother or sister in Christ, but to speak in the language of "enemy." It draws me on to ask the Lord to "grant to our enemies true peace and forgiveness of sins." What begins in anger ends in mercy and justice intermingled. I ask for true peace, which will require reconciliation through repentance.

At the end of every Confession, I resolve to avoid sin and the near occasion of sin, and it's prayers like this that help me swerve back when I'm beginning to be overwhelmed by my own errors. It's the kind of prayer I want to teach my daughter, so she's not tempted to hide from God when she makes a mistake, but to rush toward him, ready to be healed.

By the end of the prayer, by the grace of God, I'm no longer Bombaloo.

Lord, Help Me to Love

Lord Jesus Christ, who didst command us to love our enemies, and those who defame and injure us, and to pray for them and forgive them; who thyself didst pray for thine enemies who crucified thee:

Grant us, we pray, the spirit of Christian reconciliation and meekness, that we may heartily forgive every injury and be reconciled with our enemies. Grant us to overcome the malevolence and offences of people with Christian meekness and true love of our neighbor.

We further beseech thee, O Lord, to grant to our enemies true peace and forgiveness of sins; do not allow them to leave this life without true faith and sincere conversion. And help us repay evil with goodness, and to remain safe from the temptations of the devil and from all the perils which threaten us, in the form of visible and invisible enemies. Amen.[5]

THE AVE PRAYER BOOK FOR CATHOLIC MOTHERS

Entrusting Our Troubles to Our Lady

Marge Steinhage Fenelon

More than a decade ago, our pastor talked about the Novena to Our Lady, Undoer of Knots, in a Sunday homily. He told us that the devotion dated back to the 1600s when a German nobleman named Wolfgang Langenmantel was having difficulty in his marriage and sought the counsel of a wise priest. Back then, it was a German custom to gently bind the hands of the bride and groom with a silk ribbon during the wedding ceremony. The priest asked Wolfgang to bring his marriage ribbon to their next meeting.

Over the years, the ribbon had accumulated a number of twists and knots that were impossible to untie. So the priest presented the ribbon to Our Lady, and the knots miraculously disappeared. Through this miracle, Wolfgang and his wife were reunited and lived a long and happy life together. The devotion to Our Lady, Undoer of Knots, spread from there.

Our pastor urged us to try this powerful novena for ourselves. Skeptical and a bit curious, I decided to take up the challenge. What happened was astounding. Immediately after I began the novena, I was overcome with a deep peace and an inexplicable confidence that everything would be okay. It was as if I could tangibly feel Mary loosening the knots in the ribbon of my life. Each time I pray the novena, my conviction grows. You can find the novena on various websites; below is my own prayer to Mary under this extraordinary title.

Prayer to Undo the Knots of My Life

Our Lady, Undoer of Knots, no one knows the knots in my life as you do. No one understands my troubled heart as you do. For me, these knots are impossible to untangle, but you can undo them because your wisdom and grace are limitless. I need only to entrust the knotted ribbon of my life to you, yet I hesitate because of my stubbornness and lack of faith.

Our Lady, help me to trust in you. Help me to let go of this snarled ribbon so that you can work miracles in my life as only you can. Take the ribbon of my life from my hands and give me the grace to surrender it to you and to wait patiently as you work through each knot, one at a time. Return the ribbon only after you have undone the knots, and never again let me hold it entirely on my own. Hold onto it with me always, dear mother. Amen.

THE AVE PRAYER BOOK FOR CATHOLIC MOTHERS

COPING WITH REJECTION

Patrice Fagnant-MacArthur

When one of my biological sons was a little boy, he went through a phase when he told me every day that I was the worst mother ever and that he hated me. Every day I would respond, "I know. I still love you." Thankfully, he outgrew that phase, and we now have a close relationship.

Even that difficult phase could not prepare me for the times when my adopted daughter completely rejects me. It comes from a place of grief. She loves and misses her biological mother, even though I have been the one who has physically cared for her since she was four months old. She grieves the life she lost.

In a perfect world, there would be no such thing as adoption. All children would grow up safe and loved by their biological parents. I don't know why my daughter's heart had to be broken the day she was born, but I do know that the trauma is real and that the only person who can truly heal her is God. While I acknowledge her pain and love her even when my own heart stings from the rejection, I pray for God to heal the brokenness inside of her.

Jesus knew rejection. As he hung on the Cross, he prayed, "Father, forgive them; for they know not what they do" (Lk 23:34). When our children reject us, we need to pray for them to know that God loves them and that we love them.

In the struggle to make authentic connections with children and teens who have been traumatized by the loss of one or both biological parents, this powerful intercessory prayer can be a source of grace, as Jesus works quietly behind the scenes to bring healing and hope into troubled family dynamics. I offer this prayer daily for my adopted daughter.

Healing Prayer to the Sacred Heart

O Lord, Jesus Christ, to Your Most Sacred Heart I confide this intention: Please heal my daughter (son) in all the ways that she (he) needs to be healed. Help her (him) to love and to trust and to know that she (he) is loved. Help her (him) to make good decisions and be the person You want her (him) to be.

Only look upon me, then do what Your Heart inspires. Let Your Sacred Heart decide.

I count on You. I trust in You. I throw myself on Your mercy.

Lord Jesus! You will not fail me. Sacred Heart of Jesus, I trust in You.

Sacred Heart of Jesus, I believe in Your love for me.

Sacred Heart of Jesus, Your Kingdom Come.

O Sacred Heart of Jesus, I have asked for many favors, but I earnestly implore this one. Take it, place it in Your Sacred Heart.

When the Eternal Father sees it covered with Your Precious Blood, He will not refuse it. It will no longer be my prayer but Yours, O Jesus.

O Sacred Heart of Jesus, I place my trust in You. Let me never be confounded. Amen.[6]

Thank God Ahead of Time

Allison Gingras

Seemingly overnight, eczema had erupted all over my body. Middle age had proved to be more difficult than I anticipated. This latest malady became my tipping point, especially the challenge of navigating motherhood without always having full use of my hands.

As I worked through various treatments, I unleashed extra prayer into my health battles. During this time, I discovered Bl. Solanus Casey (1870–1957) and was drawn to his faith, humility, and simple, prayerful life. A humble doorkeeper at St. Bonaventure Monastery in Detroit, he was known in his lifetime as a wonder-worker and healer. During the Great Depression, he organized a soup kitchen to meet the needs of thousands of desperate men and women who came to him, above all, for the nourishment of their souls. He was beatified by Pope Francis in 2017.

Solanus served God and people tirelessly, regardless of the many challenges he faced. He believed one should continually offer God a grateful heart and taught those who came to him for advice to "thank God ahead of time" in every circumstance, regardless of how our prayers end up being answered.

When I learned that Solanus also struggled with chronic eczema, he secured a place in my "saint posse." The simple prayer below is a juxtaposition of two of his most famous sayings.

A Simple Prayer of Trust

Blessed be God in all his designs.
I thank you, Lord, ahead of time.
Blessed Solanus Casey, pray for me.

Lifting Up Our Service Members

Elizabeth A. Tomlin

My husband, Greg, went to college on an ROTC scholarship and was commissioned into the army on May 12, 2001. Just four months later, the attacks of September 11, 2001, forever influenced the trajectory of his service. Greg has spent years deployed between peacekeeping operations in Kosovo and combat operations in Iraq and a good bit of time on unaccompanied tour in South Korea.

In his nearly twenty years of service, military life has taught us to cherish the time that our family spends together, to take care of the soldiers and families in our army unit, and to pray without ceasing for peace in our world and for the safety of those who serve in the profession of arms.

One day, when my friend Lynda MacFarland—a United States Army wife and mom—was driving home from a memorial service for a young soldier who had been killed in action, she felt compelled to pray particularly for service members and military families. Upon arriving home, she wrote the Rosary for Warriors.

Military life carries with it pride in serving our nation but also some apprehension because the work of a service member is inherently dangerous. As a military spouse, I have found that praying the Rosary for Warriors, based on the Sorrowful Mysteries of the Rosary, helps me to place my personal anxiety at the foot of the Cross and to entrust my husband (and all service members and our nation) to God's holy will.

The Rosary for Warriors

Focus on the following intentions while praying the Sorrowful Mysteries of the Rosary.

1. *The Agony in the Garden:* We pray for deployed service members and their safety.
2. *The Scourging at the Pillar:* We pray for the healing of wounded service members.
3. *The Crowning with Thorns:* We pray for the repose of deceased service members.

4. *The Carrying of the Cross:* We pray for families of deployed, wounded, and deceased service members, and for strength and comfort.

5. *The Crucifixion:* We pray for our nation, for the victims of war, and for peace in the world.

When Adult Children Move Back Home

Kendra Von Esh

My stepchildren's mother passed away in 2017, in a sudden and tragic turn of events. Our lives were forever changed, but it became one of the brightest blessings as we all walked into a new life together. My husband's two sons, both in their early twenties, brought their two dogs into our home, and our instant family flourished. My husband and I were grateful for this opportunity as we said to each other, "It's our turn!"

Our house quickly turned into a home filled with laughter and conversation. We got to know one another on a different level—adults helping adults with adult issues. We were there through their personal relationships, gave them guidance in their career decisions, and loved them through some breakups.

My husband was a permanent father figure and taught them practical life skills with household projects. I was a beacon of spiritual light during this time as I left my executive career to begin my ministry. Our conversations grew deeper toward God, spirituality, and faith. If they had not come to live with us, I am not sure these heartfelt moments would have happened.

Even though it was a big adjustment, we all believe it was the best thing that could have happened. The young men have since moved out, but we all agreed to "get the band back together" once a month—with the dogs! Thank you, God, for this great blessing!

Lord, Make My Heart a Welcoming Place

Lord, please purify my heart—make it clean, contrite, and new.
Mother Mary, wrap me in your mantle so I can love like you.
Jesus, give me your heart so I can cherish those you put in my care.
Holy Spirit, pour out your gifts so I can love always and everywhere.
Amen.

Your Love Is Sweeter than Wine

Erica Campbell

There was a time in my life when alcohol was my go-to coping mechanism to deal with the darkness I was experiencing. Getting sober was what I describe as a pure moment of grace. It was light illuminating the dark recesses of my soul that had been covered in shame and guilt. As I quit drinking, I quickly learned that the only cure for alcoholism was turning my will and my life over to God. It required and continues to require God's grace and taking things one day at a time.

When the darkness returns, when it all feels too much, when depression sets in, it is that same grace that I need to wash over me. When all seems lost or when I crumble from the exhaustion of motherhood and running a business, when the events of the world around me feel like too much to bear, I beg for the light of Christ to return.

This is my prayer for when I need to remember that God's love is my heart's delight, the one thing that sustains and heals. May this prayer be of help to you, too.

O Lord, My Sweetness and My Light

Lord, everything feels so dark and lonely.
I can't seem to find you through the fog that has covered my life.
I know that you are all-loving and all-powerful.
Send your Holy Spirit to cover me in your grace. It is the only hope for me.
I cannot do this on my own and desperately need your goodness.
Shed your light into the darkest corners of my soul
so that I may be light for others.
You are mine, and I am yours.
Amen.

PART VI

PRAYERS FOR
WHILE YOU WORK

"Establish the work of our hands."
Psalm 90:17

However we spend our days—working outside of the home to support our families, staying at home with our children, or volunteering at church or in the community—all that we are and all that we have belong to God, and are expressions of our primary vocation, "a vocation to holiness and to the mission of evangelizing the world" (*CCC* 1533).

So much of what we do as wives and mothers is hidden from all but the most observant eyes, and yet it does not go unseen by the One who loves us most. And so, we can persevere, knowing that God will provide everything we need to accomplish what he wants us to do.

In the pages that follow, you will find prayers that will encourage and strengthen you to face particular challenges. Be confident that when we ask, the Lord will indeed "establish the work of our hands" (Ps 90:17).

Changing Our Perspective

Michele Faehnle

When my children were all little, I adapted one of their preschool songs to describe my household tasks. It went like this:

> Hurry, hurry, do the dishes,
> Hurry, hurry, fold the laundry,
> Hurry, hurry, pick the kids up,
> Then start over again.

I added in other lines when making dinner, scrubbing toilets, sweeping the floor, changing diapers, and performing many of the other daily chores I had to do in addition to my job as a nurse. It was exhausting, thankless work that I did not enjoy.

It was about that time that I began reading the *Diary of Saint Faustina Maria Kowalska,* a Polish sister who received extraordinary visions of Jesus and chronicled them in her *Diary.* This saint is most known for the image Jesus instructed her to have painted: the risen Christ, standing with one arm raised in blessing, the other pulling back his garment to reveal pale and red rays emanating from his heart. Below the image are transcribed the words, "Jesus, I trust in You."

Reading the *Diary,* I began to learn more about the devotion to Divine Mercy, a radical call to live a life transformed by mercy, and about Jesus' desire to have the message of mercy spread throughout the world. St. Faustina was a simple sister whose daily tasks included cooking, cleaning, gardening, washing clothes, and answering the door at the convent. She offered all her difficult little sacrifices throughout her day to Jesus, as if they were a beautiful bouquet of flowers.

This is one of my favorite prayers from the *Diary.* It has helped me change my perspective on the mundane tasks of motherhood, allowing them to help transform me into a vessel of mercy.

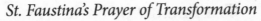

St. Faustina's Prayer of Transformation

O Most Holy Trinity! As many times as I breathe, as many times as my heart beats, as many times as my blood pulsates through my body, so many thousand times do I want to glorify Your mercy.

I want to be completely transformed into Your mercy and to be Your living reflection, O Lord. May the greatest of all divine attributes, that of Your unfathomable mercy, pass through my heart and soul to my neighbor.

Help me, O Lord, that my eyes may be merciful, so that I may never suspect or judge from appearances but look for what is beautiful in my neighbors' souls and come to their rescue.

Help me, that my ears may be merciful, so that I may give heed to my neighbors' needs and not be indifferent to their pains and moanings.

Help me, O Lord, that my tongue may be merciful, so that I should never speak negatively of my neighbor but have a word of comfort and forgiveness for all.

Help me, O Lord, that my hands may be merciful and filled with good deeds, so that I may do only good to my neighbors and take upon myself the more difficult and toilsome tasks.

Help me, that my feet may be merciful, so that I may hurry to assist my neighbor, overcoming my own fatigue and weariness. My true rest is in the service of my neighbor.

Help me, O Lord, that my heart may be merciful so that I myself may feel all the sufferings of my neighbor. I will refuse my heart to no one. I will be sincere even with those who, I know, will abuse my kindness. And I will lock myself up in the most merciful Heart of Jesus. I will bear my own suffering in silence.

May Your mercy, O Lord, rest upon me.[1]

THE SECRET OF SANCTITY

Dorothy Pilarski

Each of us reaches milestones in our journey of faith. We have all experienced moments, met people, and found prayers (or scripture passages) that we will never forget. They leave indelible marks on our soul. The year my father died suddenly and unexpectedly in Poland (while on holiday) was such a time for me. I was twenty-four and considered myself "Daddy's little girl." The profound grief and desperation I felt in losing my dad galvanized my commitment to attend daily Mass.

As a woman in my twenties raised in an aggressively feminist culture, I doubted that God had a plan for me. I was indoctrinated to believe, "If it was to be, it was all up to me." It was a painful and confusing time. Born in Poland and raised by two devout parents, I was strongly immersed in Catholic culture. Yet like so many women my age, I questioned everything the Church taught.

I can't remember exactly when I stumbled on a prayer card with the Prayer to the Holy Spirit by Cardinal Désiré-Joseph Mercier (1851–1926). This prayer, printed below, forever changed the course of my life. It struck something deep within me. Whether making decisions while traveling on business internationally or discerning what to do as a wife and mother, I have prayed that prayer. It's posted on my refrigerator. I have printed and distributed thousands of copies of Cardinal Mercier's Holy Spirit prayer, along with his suggestions about how to pray it. I know you will be blessed by it, too.

Prayer to the Holy Spirit

I am going to reveal to you the secret of sanctity and happiness. Every day for five minutes control your imagination and close your eyes to the things of sense and your ears to all the noises of the world, in order to enter into yourself. Then, in the sanctity of your baptized soul (which is the temple of the Holy Spirit), speak to that Divine Spirit, saying to him:

"Oh, Holy Spirit, beloved of my soul, I adore You. Enlighten me, guide me, strengthen me, console me. Tell me what I should do. Give me your orders. I promise to submit myself to all that You desire of me and accept all that You will permit to happen to me. Let me only know Your Will."

If you do this, your life will flow along happily, serenely, and full of consolation, even in the midst of trials. Grace will be proportioned to the trial, giving you strength to carry it, and you will arrive at the gate of Paradise laden with merit. This submission to the Holy Spirit is the secret of sanctity.[2]

Lean into the Chaos

Kathryn Whitaker

A priest once told me to stop praying like a nun and start praying like a mom. So good, right? The word "prayer" often summons an image of a church pew, a quiet spot in your house, or a serene outdoor setting. But, y'all. I have six kids—college to kindergarten—and nothing about that says "conducive to prayer." So, lean into the chaos it is.

As a former evangelical Protestant, most of my prayers are spontaneous aside from the Lord's Prayer (the Our Father) and the Doxology ("Praise God, from whom all blessings flow . . ."). They almost always originate from a good praise-and-worship song, with my hands in the air and eyes closed. Remember, prayer is just you having a conversation with Jesus. No more, no less.

Sometimes I begin my day with the Morning Offering (which is beautiful, by the way), and sometimes it's a simple, "Jesus, fix it." The one task that I am always charged with is washing dishes, mornings and evenings, and sometimes in between. My prayer space is filled with whiskey low balls, cutting boards, and knives. I'm almost always listening to my dishwashing prayer list on Spotify, pink-gloved hands deep in hot, soapy water and a heart fully present to Jesus. It's a precious pocket of time with God, and the kids have learned to let me be.

Let Jesus find you in the chaos each morning, even if your prayer space isn't picture-perfect. He's got a cup of hot tea waiting (you're just gonna have to wash it when he's done).

A Kitchen Sink Offering

O Jesus, through the Immaculate Heart of Mary, I offer you my prayers, works, joys, and sufferings of this day for all the intentions of your Sacred Heart, in union with the Holy Sacrifice of the Mass throughout the world, for the salvation of souls, the reparation of sins, the reunion of all Christians, and in particular for the intentions of the Holy Father this month. Amen.

Enlisting Angelic Help

Theresa Thomas

The Catholic Church teaches that from the moment of conception until death, each person is assigned a guardian angel by God. St. Basil the Great said, "Beside each believer stands an angel as protector and shepherd leading him to life" (*CCC* 336). The angels are created, non-corporeal (no body) beings that help us avoid spiritual dangers and get to heaven. The old *Baltimore Catechism* tells us that we are made to know, love, and serve God in this world, so that we can be with God in the next. A guardian angel's sole purpose is to guide a person in this goal. How fortunate we are to have this advocate, this friend, this strong presence and gift of God's love beside us day and night!

St. Padre Pio could see not only his own but others' guardian angels. He advised his spiritual daughter, "For the love of God, do not forget this invisible companion who is always present to listen to you and always ready to console you."[3]

Let us invoke not only our guardian angels daily but also the angels of our dear children, who are with them always, even when we cannot be. Let us turn our children over to their angels' loving care, and ask the angels to protect and lead them through the dangers of life.

A Maternal Prayer to the Guardian Angels

I humbly salute ye, O ye faithful, heavenly Friends of my children! I give ye heartfelt thanks for all the love and goodness ye show them. At some future day I shall, with thanks more worthy than I can now give, repay your care for them; and before the whole heavenly court acknowledge their indebtedness to your guidance and protection. Continue to watch over them. Provide for all their needs of body and soul. Pray, likewise, for me, for my husband, and for my whole family that we may all one day rejoice in your blessed society. Amen.[4]

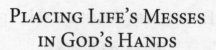

PLACING LIFE'S MESSES IN GOD'S HANDS

Rebecca Frech

I am a novena girl, ever since coming back to the faith. Spending nine days in prayer and conversation with God about whatever is on my mind or heart creates a soothing rhythm that boosts my faith. I love stretching myself to make it to the end, like running a spiritual marathon. I love all novenas . . . until the third day when I suddenly remember I should be on the prayer for day eight, and sigh in resignation as I resolve to begin again.

When a friend of mine told me about the Nine Annoying Things Novena, I fell in love with the idea of it. It's super fast and easy, and all the things that would normally pull my focus away from prayer actually become a part of it. It's the perfect prayer for busy mothers. I find that the more I offer up, the less irritated I become as I place life's messes straight into God's hands.

These annoyances don't have to be as big as the dog scarfing down the Thanksgiving turkey and then puking it back up again on the rug. Burning a casserole or listening to your eight-year-old's running monologue on all things Minecraft will work just fine. All those trifling things that create a steady drip, drip, drip of torture on your brain? Give them as a gift to God. I've heard that all things are lovely in his sight, so that must include my toddler painting the bathroom with my new waterproof mascara or the baby cussing in front of my mother-in-law. Right?

If your day is awful, you might fly through nine things in five minutes (look how much God loves you, you lucky girl!), and then you can begin another novena right away. If it takes a little longer, that's okay too. Remember, this is a no-time-limit novena!

At the beginning of the day offer this prayer of intention, and as the day progresses and "life happens," simply offer up the next nine things that vex you with as much calmness and humility as you can muster.

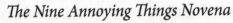

The Nine Annoying Things Novena

Heavenly Father, I know that all things are wonderful in your sight, but right now I'm not sure that I agree. Life is weighing heavily on me today, and my patience and endurance are being sorely tested. These trials may not be large or complicated, but all of them together feel like more weight than I can carry right now, and so I am giving them as a gift to you.

I offer up to you the next nine things that cause me annoyance or frustration, or that try my patience. I accept them humbly and calmly as part of your great plan for me, and I willingly submit to your will. Take these nine things as my living prayer for _____ (intention). I pray also that you would allow me to see the good in these nine irritations and understand how all things are according to your will.

In Jesus' name I pray. Amen.

The Blessing of Social Media

Kitty Cleveland

Like many busy and distracted Catholic moms, I had always struggled to pray the Rosary consistently. It wasn't until the pandemic canceled most of my outside commitments that my teenage daughter, Cecilia, and I started praying the Rosary every evening together. We came to love it.

Then, this year while I was praying in my parish's perpetual adoration chapel on the Feast of the Assumption, I was prompted to start a 54-day Rosary novena, live on social media. I had never made such a long prayer commitment, but that wasn't the tough part: The Rosary was to begin at *6:00 in the morning*!

I was practically sleepwalking the next morning when I arose at 5:30, letting my daughter sleep until 5:45. We started the live video on Facebook, and we were astounded as we watched the numbers climb. Eighty people showed up that first day, and as the weeks went by, the number climbed into the hundreds. So many people were craving authentic community; joining us in prayer allowed them to connect in a way that was both safe and intentional. The fruit was so abundant that we committed to continue to pray the Rosary daily even after the official novena ended.

The whole experience reminded me of something Pope Francis said in his 2014 address for the 48th World Communications Day: "Media can help us to feel closer to one another, creating a sense of the unity of the human family which can in turn inspire solidarity and serious efforts to ensure a more dignified life for all. . . . The internet . . . offers immense possibilities for encounter and solidarity. This is something truly good, a gift from God."[5]

Opening Prayer for the Online Rosary

Heavenly Father, St. Thérèse of Lisieux said that the Rosary is a long chain that links heaven and earth. The links of this chain bind our hearts to the Sacred Heart of Jesus and to the Immaculate Heart of our Blessed Mother. May they also bind our hearts to one another, in joy and sorrow, in times of blessing and adversity.

Thank you, Lord, for the blessing of social media. Help me to use it wisely. As I pray this online Rosary, may Our Lady take me by the hand and teach me how to shoulder the burdens of others. Help me to connect with others and to become a force of goodness, encouragement, and peace in this aching world. By the Holy Spirit, guide our meditations as we mine the riches of each mystery, so they may bear abundant fruit in our lives.

Our Lady, Queen of the Rosary and Queen of Peace, pray for us. Amen.

Made in the Image of God
Kate Wicker

Like so many women, I have a complicated relationship with my body. As a child, I was tenant to a larger body and was teased and called names like "Miss Piggy." Later my body became a weapon I wielded against myself and my constant, ever-failing quest to be perfect and in control. I succumbed to an eating disorder. I worked long and hard at recovery and eventually began to see my body more as an instrument than an object to be picked apart. Pregnancy, nursing, bear hugs, chasing errant children, cooking meals with my hands—all the tasks of motherhood, even the most menial, such as folding laundry—revealed that God created my body with the purpose to love and to serve. I had so much more to offer the world than skin.

And yet, there are still days when I catch a glimpse of myself in the mirror or feel the softness of my belly that has come with middle age and five pregnancies, and I'm tempted to fixate on my perceived flaws and use my body as a scapegoat for all that I don't like about myself.

But I'm learning to step away from the mirror or the scale and to turn to God instead. The *Catechism* says that "prayer restores [us] to God's likeness" (*CCC* 2572). We are made in the image and likeness of God, not Hollywood or some snazzy Snapchat filter. We become more like him, not by going on yet another diet or obsessing over every inch of our skin, but by spending more time with him.

Lord, Thank You for My Motherly Body

Dear Lord, thank you for the gift of motherhood. Help me to love the way you have molded my body for motherhood. My body is a miracle to be praised. Maker of all things, help me to see my body, not as an object to be consumed or tweaked, but as an instrument to do your work—to nurture and to bring life into the world, whether through physical birth, adoption, or as a spiritual mother.

Give me the eyes to appreciate wider hips for carrying tired children, a softer tummy for pillowing their heads, the miracle of my fingers—how they can pick up a pen and write a letter to a loved one or make a small child feel secure by enclosing her tiny hand—and my heart, a strong muscle that works day and night and provides a soothing symphony for all who rest their head upon my chest.

Lord, I'm so thankful for your design of my body even if it doesn't fit into any cultural ideal. Use my children, my life, my purpose to shape me into your image. Use motherhood as a means for me to grow in sacrificial love. Use my children's clinging arms to make me more generous. Use their giggles and spontaneous hugs to make me more aware of the joy of my vocation. Use their neediness to make me more compassionate.

My heavenly Creator, use my body, my soul, my entire being, not only to be a better mother, but also to do your will. I am beautiful in every way because of you. Amen.

Accompanying Our
Elderly Parents

Lisa M. Hendey

As a woman in active ministry, I thought I had a fairly good understanding of the many and varied ways that God calls us to emulate Mary's fiat by giving our own faith-filled yes to his will for our lives. But it wasn't until my own mother's journey into Parkinson's disease and related dementia began to challenge our family in unforeseen ways that I really learned to walk my talk. In so many ways, accompanying my parents along their precipitous path of aging has sent me to my knees figuratively and literally.

As I type these words, Mom has entered the hospice phase of her earthly journey. Every night before I drift off to sleep, I ask God to hold his daughter Anne, my precious mother, in his arms in those moments when I physically cannot. I beg God to bring her peace and solace, to ease her physical and emotional pain, and to minister to her through the hands of her caregivers.

Mom is now largely nonverbal, apart from a garbled version of the Hail Mary that is her only form of speech. Yet she continues to teach me daily what it truly means to love God by loving others. I love that her instinct is to pray for us all, now and at the hour of death. I have every confidence that when Mom's earthly journey ends, she will spend her eternity in God's embrace, praying for us as she has always done. Until that moment, I beg God often for the courage to trust his perfect plan and for the grace to cherish Mom while she is with us.

This prayer was inspired by my experience of caring for my own parents. I hope it will inspire and encourage others in their caregiving journey.

A Caregiver's Prayer

Loving Father, I offer into the warmth of your embrace your beloved children, my parents *(names)*. While they remain with us in this life, I ask you for the means, courage, and empathy to lovingly provide for their mental, physical, emotional, and spiritual care. Embolden me to advocate effectively on their behalf. Bless all of those who serve as their caretakers and let them minister to my parents with skill, wisdom, and compassion.

Through this simple prayer, I lift my loved ones into your arms, God. Calm my busy mind and help me to listen patiently. Help me to ease their pain, calm their fears, affirm their dignity, and above all to reassure them that they are cherished and loved.

Thank you for the gift they have been in my life and for the lessons they have taught me, and for the sense of purpose, mission, and faith they instilled in me. Whether I must love them from a distance or care for their daily needs, show me how to love them as they need to be loved. Give me your grace to see the face of your Son Jesus in their eyes. In the name of the Father, and the Son, and the Holy Spirit. Amen.

LIFT THEM UP TO JESUS

Katie Prejean McGrady

When I was a teacher, I often found myself exhausted at the end of a school day. Having spent hours repeating the same material, class after class, I'd usually go home, collapse on my couch, watch reruns of whatever happened to be on basic cable, and take a nap.

Burnt out didn't even begin to capture how I felt, and I randomly expressed my exhaustion to a student's mom one afternoon. She swung by school to pick up some paperwork, saw me walking to my car, asked me how I was, and I randomly unloaded. (Fortunately, she and I knew each other outside of school, so I wasn't just holding a self-proclaimed pity party with a stranger.) She patiently listened to me, gave me a hug, and offered a word of advice. "Take care of yourself. Take a mental health day if you need it." And then she said something beautiful. "And know that I'm praying for you."

We often say that—*I'm praying for you*. But in this instance, I knew she meant it.

A few days later, a card was sitting in my teacher mailbox in the coffee room. It was from this mom. In it was a Starbucks gift card and a note. "Katie, I've been praying these words for you ever since we talked. Know that I'm lifting you up to Jesus." Beneath that line she had written out the words to her prayer, which I share with you here.

I was moved to tears, and her card still sits on my desk—though now I pray those words for my own child's teachers.

Prayer for My Child's Teachers

Lord, give strength, courage, wisdom, and patience to my child's teachers.

Comfort them when they are tired.

Guide them when they are lost.

Help them to be your hands and feet to the students they meet and teach.

I ask this, in the most holy name of Jesus.

Amen.

CALLED TO WRITE
Michelle Buckman

Writing in the pre-internet days was no easy task. We writers felt totally isolated, especially those of us stuck in small towns without writing groups.

Despite the lack of support, I felt God's urging and forged ahead, finally writing a saleable manuscript after many, many failed attempts. However, after several successful novels, my agent, who was with the Christian Booksellers Association, rejected my fifth book, *Rachel's Contrition*, because of the blatant Catholicism I wove into the plot.

I didn't know what to do. Without an agent, how could I land another publishing contract? I had already been rejected by New York publishers for mild Christian references.

I twisted and turned in my prayers before God, seeking some sign as to whether I should completely remove faith from my writing and revise my next book to sell in the secular market.

As the war waged in my subconscious, God gave me a clear answer.

A woman at church approached me after Mass and dragged me to a distant corner of the parking lot. "I read your book," she said. "*My Beautiful Disaster.*"

I tensed. "Did you like it?"

She stared at me for a very long moment before speaking. "I'm pregnant and I haven't been sure what to do. But now, after reading your novel, I have decided I'm keeping my baby."

Her words went straight to my heart—including faith in my stories *did* matter!

God doesn't always provide such an obvious answer, but he is listening and will guide us if we seek his counsel.

A Writer's Prayer

Lord, I need your help today as I stare at this blank page. I know you placed me on this road in life, pen in hand, because you have a plan. You know the words I am called to write and the readers you intend to reach. You already know whose lives out there in the world need a revelation that may be sparked by a character or story or reflection or article, even while I am writing blindly according to what you put on my heart. Help me today, Lord, to focus on the work you've put before me. Help me to heed your urgings. Guide me, Lord, that I may accomplish good works through you and for your everlasting glory. Amen.

THE AVE PRAYER BOOK FOR CATHOLIC MOTHERS

Soul of a Woman

Christina Dehan Jaloway

I first fell in love with the writings of Edith Stein (aka St. Teresa Benedicta of the Cross) when I was in grad school and read her *Essays on Woman* with some girlfriends during Lent. I decided to reread the essays a few months ago and was struck by this passage about the soul of a woman: "The relationship of soul and body is different in man and woman; the relationship of soul to body differs in their psychic life as well as that of the spiritual faculties to each other. The feminine species expresses a unity and wholeness of the total psychosomatic personality and a harmonious development of the faculties."[6]

This prayer was inspired by Edith Stein's reflections.

Lord, Complete Your Creation

Lord, please help me become the woman you created me to be.

Expand my soul so that nothing human is alien to me. Prompt me to search for and bring home the hidden treasures and burdens that rest in every human soul. Send me to the souls who most need what you have given me.

Quiet my soul, so that no weak flame of faith, hope, or charity may be extinguished by stormy winds. Let my soul be a place where the weak and suffering may find refuge and solace.

Warm my soul with the heavenly fire of your divine love. Consume and purify the worldly, chaotic fire within me so that I may be a clear sign of your love in the world. With clarity, grant me simplicity of heart that, with Mary, I will always choose the better part, which will not be taken from me.

Empty me of my agitated, unredeemed self, so that I may have room in my heart for others. Help me to remember that you are the only one who is capable of receiving me completely so that I may joyfully surrender to you.

Give me the grace to be self-contained, to be mistress of myself as a handmaid of the Lord, prepared to serve all whom you desire me to serve, and to submit to the authorities you have placed over me.

Above all, help me to realize that my natural desire to give myself completely to someone can only be fulfilled in relationship with you.

St. Teresa Benedicta of the Cross, pray for us. Amen.

PART VII

PRAYERS FOR PEACE IN TIMES OF GRIEF AND LOSS

~∽◦∽~

"Love is strong as death."
Song of Solomon 8:6

In the forge of grief and loss our hearts are expanded and purified, making us more compassionate and tender in this life . . . and shaping us to long for the eternal reunion in the next.

These prayers arise from the reality of this kind of loss, as well as the certainty that this is not the end, that more and better is in store. In the words of the Song of Solomon, "Set me as a seal upon your heart, as a seal upon your arm; for love is strong as death, jealousy is cruel as the grave. Its flashes are flashes of fire, a most vehement flame" (8:6).

Our Lady of Sorrows, pray for us.

God's Mercy Never Ends
Trisha Short

The greater the sinner, the greater the right he has to My mercy.
—*Diary of Saint Faustina Maria Kowalska, #723*

Twenty-five years ago, a compassionate pro-life friend introduced me to the Chaplet of Divine Mercy to help me begin the process of healing from two early abortions. I wasn't a practicing Catholic at the time, but reciting it for the first time brought a deep contrition that led me running to Confession and back into the Catholic Church.

The Chaplet of Divine Mercy is a powerhouse prayer of atonement for the many evils of sin. I have seen Jesus' promises to St. Faustina proven again and again in offering the chaplet both for the conversion of hardened sinners and at the bedside of the dying. Praying it for my parents and my son in their dying hours, I witnessed Jesus extending a miraculous final grace to their dying souls.

As women, we are called to be stewards of the generations. We are daughters, sisters, wives, mothers, grandmothers, cousins, aunts, and friends. Through our faithful recitation of the chaplet, let us intercede for our families and our world. May we reap many souls for the kingdom of God, especially the souls of our loved ones.

As recorded in St. Faustina's *Diary*, the Lord said to her, "**encourage souls to say the chaplet which I have given to you**" (#1541). And "**whoever will recite it will receive great mercy at the hour of death**" (#687). Let us especially offer this chaplet at the bedside of a dying loved one.

Chaplet of Divine Mercy

Begin by making the Sign of the Cross.

Then say the Our Father, Hail Mary, and Apostles' Creed.

On the large ("Our Father") beads, pray: Eternal Father, I offer you the Body and Blood, Soul and Divinity of Your Dearly Beloved Son, Our Lord Jesus Christ, in atonement for our sins and those of the whole world.

On the small ("Hail Mary") beads, pray: For the sake of His sorrowful Passion, have mercy on us and on the whole world.

Concluding prayer (Repeat 3 times): Holy God, Holy Mighty One, Holy Immortal One, have mercy on us and on the whole world.

Optional closing prayer: Eternal God, in whom mercy is endless and the treasury of compassion inexhaustible, look kindly upon us and increase Your mercy in us, that in difficult moments we might not despair nor become despondent, but with great confidence submit ourselves to Your holy will, which is Love and Mercy itself. Amen.

BIRTH INTO NEW LIFE

Annabelle Moseley

In the third trimester of pregnancy, you can gently press on your stomach and your unborn child will return the press. This touch is nothing like the close embrace that awaits once the child is born, but it's a beautiful foretaste.

There are ways that God touches us now, and just as an unborn child senses there is something *beyond* that they want to get to . . . we trust there is something beyond this world, too.

As mothers and women of faith, we can find hope in the realization that death is another kind of labor, the kind that assists in bringing forth new life in God. Let us think of our final perseverance as a labor through which we are born to eternal life. And let us impart strong faith in our children, reminding them that just as they didn't know what awaited them when they were babies in the womb, they must trust when they face death that new life awaits. With our last breath, may we have a childlike humility and trust as we wait to feel God's hand upon us.

This is a prayer I wrote to help us reflect on the fact that death, for those who trust in Christ, is actually birth into a new life.

A Reflection on Life and Death

Three months before your time, my child, you moved
head down into position, ripe for birth.
The world outside was unseen and unproved
but still you leaped as though you sensed its worth
and wanted it. And though your world was dark,
removed from any touch except my hand
passing above your solitary ark
you ate from my own blood; your cosmos spanned
my womb. Responding to my voice, you danced.
So someday when you're grown and faced with doubt
because of grief or age, by fear enhanced

remember how you once moved toward an out
you could not see. Wait—new life will begin.
Feel God's warm hand above earth's starry skin.

My Real-Life *Pietà*

Rachel Bulman

Our first son suffers from Erb's palsy, a loss of function in his left arm due to a birthing injury. At six months he underwent his first surgery, and came out eight hours later with a "Statue of Liberty" cast that went from his waist up to his shoulders and to the end of his left arm.

On one of the many nights of rocking him to sleep in this half-body cast, I started to weep. As a convert, I had struggled to develop a relationship with the Blessed Mother, yet that night, I found myself calling out for her. "Show me how to do this," I begged. His pain was so great and my heart was so heavy. How could I do this?

I closed my eyes, and as clear as day I saw the Blessed Mother holding the body of her son, limp at the foot of the Cross. Her face was tear-stained but resilient, sorrowful but stoic, distant but intimate. In that image, I saw myself holding my son.

A few years later, after my mother died and we lost our fifth child to miscarriage, I knelt before the tabernacle, closed my eyes, and saw Our Lady again. Except this time, she wasn't holding her son. She was holding my mother, and my mother was holding our baby.

If you tour St. Peter's Basilica in Rome, you will see Michelangelo's *Pietà*. The tour guide may tell you that the statue is not to scale, that the Blessed Mother could not have held the lifeless body of her son in precisely this way—her small stature would not have been able to bear the weight. And yet the image speaks of the supernatural strength, beauty, and grace of Our Lady, qualities that shine *even more brightly* in the midst of our sorrows.

Prayer to Our Lady of Sorrows

Our Lady of Sorrows, reveal the fullness of beauty within this pain. I trust your Immaculate Heart and your motherly wisdom to guide me when the way seems rough and the journey gets weary. Above all, lead me back to my first love. When the sorrow is great and the way seems hopeless, let me gaze at you in the *Pietà*, carrying the body of our Lord, and receive the strength I need to find him again and again, even in the sorrows of this life.

Jesus Is My Best Companion

Colleen C. Mitchell

Loneliness has long been a part of my journey with the Lord. From the days when caring for young babies dominated my life and left me feeling isolated from the world, to our years of missionary service when I longed for the familiar comfortable of the place I called home and the people I cherished, I have known what it means to be surrounded by people, yet feel acutely lonely.

A couple of years ago, my divorce caused me to know loneliness at a new level, a level that has threatened to sink me at times. Yes, I have four boys who keep me running here and there, dear friends who do their very best to make sure I am cared for, and sisters who are always waiting on the other end of the phone line to remind me how deeply I am loved. Still, there is a level of intimacy and affection missing from my life that I carry as a heavy burden at times.

What I am learning, though, is that Jesus is my best companion. In him, I am known intimately and loved with the most tender affection. Prayer is where my heart can rest in being known. In prayer, I can be filled with the peace of knowing that the Lover of my Soul waits for me, and with him, I am never alone.

Prayer of a Lonely Heart

Dear Lord, people say there is a difference between being lonely and being alone. Lately, I know that reality acutely. I am surrounded by my busy life with all its comings and goings, but I feel so very lonely. Lonely for intimate companionship, lonely for affection, lonely for love. But I know what is true, Lord. And I know that you desperately want to offer me those things. Touch my heart today, Jesus. Help me see that you are enough for me. Take my tender heart into your hands and love it well. Let me be filled with you. Amen.

When You Face a Final Goodbye

Mary Ann Jepsen

Many years ago, as a young mother of toddlers in my early thirties, I volunteered with the Missionaries of Charity (Mother Teresa's sisters) in the streets of Boston. It was through them and their work with the poor and suffering that I came to love a prayer popularly attributed to Cardinal John Henry Newman (1801–1890), "Radiating Christ." It was one of Mother Teresa's favorites, and the sisters pray a version of the prayer daily, asking for Christ's assistance in fashioning them as his light and love for those to whom they minister, especially among the very sick and dying.

The approaching death of a loved one is the most difficult thing we will experience. The time we spend with them prior to death, however, can be the most blessed if we take Cardinal Newman's prayer to heart. Imagine yourself being the radiance and fragrance of Christ to your suffering loved ones when they most need it. Imagine them looking at you and seeing Jesus. Imagine that light being all his, not yours, yet it came through you.

Imagine that in the midst of your own sadness you have Jesus in you, and through you he blesses them and you. Your peace in their passing comes as pure Love. Your face may be the last one they see before his very own, and what a gift it is that he chose you for that moment! When you face final goodbyes, trust they are not final. A love such as this never dies.

Radiating Christ

Dear Jesus, help me to spread Your fragrance wherever I go. Flood my soul with Your spirit and life. Penetrate and possess my whole being so utterly that my life may only be a radiance of Yours. Shine through me, and be so in me that every soul I come in contact with may feel Your presence in my soul. Let them look up and see no longer me, but only Jesus!

Stay with me and then I shall begin to shine as You shine, so to shine as to be a light to others. The light, O Jesus, will be all from You; none of it will be mine. It will be you, shining on others through me. Let me thus praise You the way You love best, by shining on those around me.

Let me preach You without preaching, not by words but by my example, by the catching force of the sympathetic influence of what I do, the evident fullness of the love my heart bears to You.

Amen.[1]

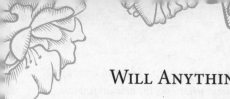

Will Anything Be Okay Again?

Andrea Remke

This "prayer" is basically the collected ramblings and musings that have been on my heart each night since my husband died. Being an anxious person, I am prone to worrying and wondering what bad things will befall me next. Some people enjoy being alone and would find the freedom of it exhilarating. I find it terrifying. I worry if I'll ever be really loved again. I worry about what effect not having a father will have on my kids. I worry about the decisions I make for us even though I'm a grown woman.

Telling these thoughts to a therapist seems weak and pointless. So instead I just ramble on about these thoughts to God, deep into the night. To be honest, though, I really don't know how to "pray." I grew up Catholic—went to church, followed the motions, said the Hail Marys, did my penance at Confession every now and then, but it never felt strong enough to really count as a "prayer." Prayer for me has become my deepest thoughts and fears, asking for help with them and then trying to give thanks for what I still have, despite my loss.

I've come to realize that the answers to what we pray for, what we ask God for, aren't always what we expect. The miracles we seek to receive via our prayers aren't always in the healing, or in the concrete "things" we seek. The miracle may be acceptance, knowing that his plan for us is beautifully designed even though we can't see it. The answer to the prayer sometimes is gaining trust in him that he will see us to our potential here—and sometimes that comes only through loss and suffering.

A Young Widow's Prayer

Dear Lord, every night I lie down, I wonder if you are there. I wonder if you can see how scared I am. Do you hear my frustrations, my anger, my exhaustion?

It's been a while now since my husband died, and I'm carrying on every day the best I can. I keep getting up and going through the motions of life as a single mother. People tell me how great I'm doing. They tell me how the kids seem happy and fine. Yes, we have our good days. But nobody but you sees the bad days. Nobody but you can see the grief I hide, the pain I mask. Because there are so many times that I want to cry out, "I'm not okay. I'm tired of being alone. I'm tired of having to do everything myself. I'm sick of wondering if I'm doing anything right. I hate worrying about the future and whether the kids will be okay not having their daddy here anymore. I miss being loved and wanted, too. Will anything ever be okay again?"

Please, Lord, help me to know you see me. Help me to know you hear my needs and desires. Teach me to be patient with the kids, with others, and with myself. Forgive my shortcomings because they are many right now. I pray, Lord, that you shower me with grace to carry on here when I feel I can't anymore.

In your name I pray. Amen.

Notes

Part I: Prayers for Encountering God

1. *Mountain Breezes: The Collected Poems of Amy Carmichael* (Fort Washington, PA: Christian Literature Crusade, 1999), 223.

2. This is an adaptation of a version found in *The Book of Catholic Prayer* (p. 259), attributed to *St. Paul Prayer Book* (UK: St. Pauls Publishing, 2012), 597.

3. From the Liturgy of the Hours, http://www.liturgies.net/Liturgies/Catholic/loh/advent/week1fridayor.htm.

4. This Act of Spiritual Communion is widely attributed to Fr. Josemaría Escrivá, founder of Opus Dei.

5. Attributed to St. Alphonsus Liguori.

6. From *The Catholic Prayer Book,* comp. Michael Buckley (Ann Arbor, MI: Servant Books, 1986), 271.

7. Francis Larkin, "Prayer for Myself," from *Enthronement of the Sacred Heart* (Boston, MA: Pauline Books and Media, 1978), 541.

8. *Oremus: A Treasury of Latin Prayers with English Translations,* trans. Christopher Bailey (Notre Dame, IN: Ave Maria Press, 2020), 27.

9. Adapted from a version available on the USCCB website, https://www.usccb.org/prayer-and-worship/prayers-and-devotions/litanies/litany-of-the-sacred-heart-of-jesus.

10. The Litany of Humility is attributed to Cardinal Merry del Val, secretary of state to Pope St. Pius X, and is taken from Fr. John Hardon, S.J., *For Jesuits* (Chicago: Loyola Press, 1963).

Part II: Prayers for Getting to Know Mary

1. Louis de Montfort, *True Devotion to Mary* (San Diego, CA: Aventine Press, 2007), 23–24.

2. Adapted from Heidi Hess Saxton, *With Mary in Prayer* (Chicago: Loyola Press, 2002), 4–5.

3. Pope John Paul II, *Rosarium Virginis Mariae,* 19, http://www.vatican.va/content/john-paul-ii/en/apost_letters/2002/documents/hf_jp-ii_apl_20021016_rosarium-virginis-mariae.html.

4. Immaculate Mary: Lourdes Hymn published in *Parochial Hymn Book, Boston, 1897; rev. of Hail Virgin of Virgins* by Jeremiah Cummings, 1814-1866. "Breaking Bread, vol 39" hymnal reproduced through Hymnary.org. https://hymnary.org/hymn/BB2020/page/252.

5. Some versions of this prayer use the word "lend" rather than "give." However, this is the original prayer St. Teresa of Calcutta taught her sisters, the Missionaries of Charity. This version is approved by the Mother Teresa Center in San Diego, California.

6. A Benedictine Monk, *In Sinu Jesus: When Heart Speaks to Heart* (Kettering, OH: Angelico Press, 2016), 269.

Part III: Prayers for a More Intimate Marriage

1. If you feel your marriage needs a bit of a "faith lift," check out Heidi's blog "Life on the Road Less Traveled" (heidisaxton.com) and sign up for her newsletter to receive a free download for her "40 Day Marriage Challenge."

2. From *Hear Me, O Lord,* Ukrainian Catholic (Byzantine) Sunday and Festal Missal.

3. As found on the EWTN website, https://www.ewtn.com/catholicism/library/novena-to-the-infant-jesus-of-prague-11875.

Part IV: Prayers of a Mother's Heart

1. This prayer of consecration can be traced to a seventeenth-century monk, Fr. Cyril, who found the original Infant of Prague statue in the carnage of the Thirty Years' War. For more information, see Fr. Joseph, M.I.C., "Consecrate Your Child to the Infant Jesus" *Marian Helper* (Winter 2003–04), https://www.marian.org/marianhelper/issues/issue230/article230294.html.

2. Adapted from the concluding prayer of Pope John Paul II in *Ecclesia in Oceania,* November 22, 2001, http://www.vatican.va/content/john-paul-ii/en/apost_exhortations/documents/hf_jp-ii_exh_20011122_ecclesia-in-oceania.html.

3. Teilhard de Chardin, "Prayer of Patient Trust" as found in *Hearts on Fire: Praying with Jesuits,* ed. Michael Harter (Chicago: Loyola Press, 2005), 102–3.

4. Elizabeth Ann Foss, *Real Learning Revisited* (2020), 27.

5. From Rev. Pius Franciscus, O.F.M.Cap., *Mother Love: A Manual for Christian Mothers,* trans. Sr. M. Agatha Scott of the Visitation Nuns (New York: Frederick Pustet Co., Inc., 1926).

6. As quoted by Fr. Jean C. J. D'Elbée in *I Believe in Love: A Personal Retreat Based on the Teaching of St. Thérèse of Lisieux* (Manchester, NH: Sophia Institute Press, 2001), 58.

Part V: Prayers for Help in Times of Trial

1. John Paul II, Apostolic Letter for the Year of the Eucharist, October 7, 2004, http://www.vatican.va/content/john-paul-ii/en/apost_letters/2004/documents/hf_jp-ii_apl_20041008_mane-nobiscum-domine.html.

2. The full text of the Chaplet of St. Michael the Archangel may be found at https://www.ewtn.com/catholicism/devotions/chaplet-of-st-michael-the-archangel-386.

3. This Morning Offertory was written in the mid-nineteenth century by Fr. François Xavier Gaulrelet for the Apostleship of Prayer, which he founded in 1844. It can be found at http://popesprayerusa.net/daily-offering-prayers/.

4. Dr. Michael J. Brescia, as quoted in the Sisters of Life Spring 2017 Newsletter, https://sistersoflife.org/wp-content/uploads/2019/05/SV-Imprint-Spring-2017.pdf.

5. Traditional prayer of the Eastern Orthodox Church.

6. Adapted from "Daily Prayers" of the Priests of the Sacred Heart, Hales Corner, Wisconsin, https://poshusa.org/prayer-resources/daily-prayer.

Part VI: Prayers While You Work

1. *Diary of Saint Maria Faustina Kowalska: Divine Mercy in My Soul* (Stockbridge, MA: Marian Press, 1987), par. 163.

2. From Cardinal Mercier, *La vie intérieure: Retraite prêchée à ses prêtres* (1923), as quoted in Jean Lafrance, *Persevering in Prayer,* trans. Florestine Audette, R.J.M. (Sherbrooke, Quebec: Médiaspaul, 2002), 77.

3. Padre Pio of Pietrelcina, in a 1914 letter to his spiritual daughter Raffaelina, as quoted in "Padre Pio and the Guardian Angel" on Free Republic: https://freerepublic.com/focus/f-religion/1495041/posts.

4. From Rev. Pius Franciscus, *Mother Love.*

5. Pope Francis, Message for the 48th World Communications Day (June 1, 2014), http://www.vatican.va/content/francesco/en/messages/communications/documents/papa-francesco_20140124_messaggio-comunicazioni-sociali.html.

6. Edith Stein, "Problems of Women's Education," in *Essays on Woman: The Collected Works of Edith Stein, Volume 2,* 2nd ed. rev. (Washington, DC: ICS Publications, 1996), 187.

Part VII: Prayers for Peace in Times of Grief and Loss

1. The original source of the italicized paragraphs can be traced to "Jesus the Light of the Soul," in *Meditations and Devotions of the Late Cardinal Newman,* Part III, VII, 3 (New York: Longmans, Green, and Co., 1893), 500.

THEMATIC INDEX

Cyril, Fr., 83

D

d'Astonac, Antonia, 119
Daunt, Carrie Schuchts, 96
death, 172–173, 176–177. *See also* grief
      and loss
DeSantis, Anne, 132
Diary of Saint Faustina Maria Kowalska,
      148, 170
discernment, 150–151
distractions, 8
domestic violence, 81–82
Dominican Rosary prayers
   about, 38
   The Apostles' Creed, 41–42
   The Fatima Prayer, 47
   The Glorious Mysteries, 56–57
   The Glory Be, 46
   The Hail Holy Queen, 48–49
   The Hail Mary, 45
   The Joyful Mysteries, 50–51
   The Luminous Mysteries, 54–55
   The Our Father, 43–44
   The Sign of the Cross, 39–40
   The Sorrowful Mysteries, 52–53

E

elderly parents, 160–161
Essays on Woman (Stein), 165

F

Fabiola, St., 81–82
Faehnle, Michele, 148–149
Fagnant-MacArthur, Patrice, 137–138
family
   in crisis, 132
   gratitude for, 97–98
   separated by distance, 63
The Fatima Prayer, 47
Fatzinger, Sam (Cecilia), 25–26, 83–84
Faustina, St., 148–149
fears, 62
Fenelon, Marge Steinhage, 119–120,
      135–136
finances, 83–84
Foss, Elizabeth Ann, 102

Francis, Pope, 139, 156
Francis, St., 68
The Franciscan Crown, 68–69
Frech, Rebecca, 39–40, 154–155
Frey, Karianna, 11–12, 17–18

G

Gaitley, Michael, 61
Gingras, Allison, 27, 139
The Glory Be, 46
Gohn, Pat, 41–42
A Grandmother's Prayer, 109
gratitude, 23, 97–98, 139
grief and loss, 48–49, 64–65, 126, 174,
      178–179
guardian angels, 153
guidance, 24
Guizar, Jenna, 116–118

H

The Hail Holy Queen, 48–49
The Hail Mary, 45
Hayes-Peirce, Sherry, 108
healing, 78–79, 170–171
Healing Prayer to the Sacred Heart,
      137–138
Helen, Sr., 58
Help Me, St. Fabiola, 81–82
Help Me to See You: A New Mother's
      Prayer, 128–129
Hendey, Lisa M., 54–55, 160–161
holy hours, 14–15
Holy Spirit, 150–151
hope, 104, 124–125
household tasks, 148–149, 152
humility, 25–26, 80
Hussem, Emily Wilson, xv–xvi
hymns, 58

I

Ignatius Loyola, St., 17
illness, 139
Immaculate Mary, 58
In Sinu Jesu, 66
infant loss, 126
Isinger, Christy, 56–57

Scripture Index

Contributors

Leticia Ochoa Adams lives outside of Austin, Texas, with her husband, three living children, two grandchildren, and three pit bulls. She is a writer and speaker whose mission is to tell as many people as possible about the God who never gave up on her, led her to the Catholic Church, and helped her through the loss of her oldest son, Anthony, to suicide in 2017. You can find her at www.leticiaoadams.com.

Mary Amore and her husband, Joe, live in Downers Grove, Illinois, and are the proud parents of two adult children and grandparents of two adorable little granddaughters. An accomplished writer and national presenter, Mary serves as the full-time executive director of Mayslake Ministries in Oakbrook Terrace, Illinois.

Jackie Francois Angel is a speaker, singer/songwriter, author, homeschooling mom, and YouTube vlogger from Orange County, California. She and her husband (and their four children) have recently become residents of the great state of Texas to work as fellows of the Word on Fire Institute.

Sherry Antonetti and her husband, Marc, live with their ten children in Gaithersburg, Maryland, where she works part-time as an English teacher in addition to being a freelance writer for the *National Catholic Register, Catholic Standard*, and Aleteia. Sherry blogs at *Chocolate for Your Brain!* when not laboring on her third book, *A Doctor a Day* (Sophia Institute Press).

Christine Kelly Baglow has been involved in a variety of lay ministries in the Church for more than three decades and is passionate about the spiritual, human, intellectual, and pastoral formation of the young. Christine recently completed a master's degree in pastoral leadership at Notre Dame Seminary in New Orleans. Her husband, Chris Baglow, is director of the Science and Religion Initiative of the McGrath Institute for Church Life at the University of Notre Dame. They have four children.

Michelle Buckman is the author of seven novels, including the award-winning *Rachel's Contrition* and *Turning in Circles*. She is also a freelance editor who works with publishers and private clients. Find her online at www.MichelleBuckman.com.

Rachel Bulman is a wife, mother, writer, and speaker. She lives in central Florida with her husband and four children. You can find out where she's speaking next at RachelBulman.com and catch her writings online at Word on Fire or Catholic Mom.

Erica Campbell is the owner and designer of Be A Heart, a Catholic lifestyle brand. She lives with her husband, Paul, and their baby Frances in San Antonio, Texas.

Sarah Christmyer is a mother of four and grandmother of five . . . and spends the time she's not with them writing and speaking about scripture and the Catholic faith. Her latest book is *Becoming Women of the Word: How to Answer God's Call with Purpose and Joy* (Ave Maria Press). Follow her blog and contact Sarah at her website, ComeIntotheWord.com.

Kitty Cleveland makes her home just outside of her native New Orleans, where she lives with her musician husband and teenage daughter/sidekick. When not in the garden or in her art studio, Kitty enjoys using her voice, through both singing and speaking, to encourage and entertain the faithful.

Stephanie Gray Connors has given more than a thousand pro-life presentations and debates over two decades in ten countries, including speaking on abortion at Google headquarters. Stephanie has authored books on abortion and assisted suicide and blogs at www.loveunleasheslife.com, from which her contribution was adapted.

Sonja Corbitt is the Bible Study Evangelista, a bestselling author and a Telly Award–winning broadcaster who teaches topical, multimedia Bible studies for Catholics. Her books include *Unleashed, Fearless, Ignite, Exalted*, and *Just Rest!*

Carrie Schuchts Daunt is a presenter and prayer minister for the John Paul II Healing Center and author of *Undone: Freeing Your Feminine Heart from the Knots of Fear and Shame.* Carrie lives with her husband, Duane, and eight kids in Tallahassee, Florida.

Anne DeSantis is a Catholic wife and mother from the Greater Philadelphia area. She and her husband, Angelo, have been married more than thirty years and have two grown daughters. Anne is a television and podcast host, a former homeschooling mother of twenty years, a Catholic author, and the director of the St. Raymond Nonnatus Foundation for Freedom, Family, and Faith. Visit her website at www.annedesantis.com.

Michele Faehnle is the codirector of the Columbus Catholic Women's Conference and the coauthor of the award-winning bestseller *Divine Mercy for Moms* as well as *The Friendship Project, Our Friend Faustina*, and *Pray Fully.* She lives in Columbus, Ohio, with her husband and four children, and works as a licensed school nurse.

Patrice Fagnant-MacArthur is the mother of two young-adult biological sons and one adopted preteen daughter. She has a master's degree in applied theology and is editor of TodaysCatholicHomeschooling.com as well as a freelance writer and editor.

Sam (Cecilia) Fatzinger is married to Rob, her high school sweetheart. Their first book, *The Catholic Guide to Spending Less and Living More,* was published by Ave Maria Press in 2021. She is a homeschool mommy to fourteen children and seven (and counting) grandbabies. Daily Mass is her oxygen.

Marge Steinhage Fenelon is the award-winning author of *Mary, Undoer of Knots: A Living Novena* and an internationally known speaker. She has written several books on Marian devotion and Catholic spirituality.

Rebecca Frech is a big-mouthed Texas girl who smokes a mean brisket and is always happy to show off her smoke rings. A self-proclaimed history nerd, she bought a house behind the town library in order to support her book-a-night reading habit. When she's not cooking, gabbing, or reading, she spends her free time raising nine children, remodeling her historic home, and sneaking off to the gym to lift all the things.

Karianna Frey is an educator, speaker, and author, living in Minnesota with her husband, Steve, and their four kids. A lover of Jesus, bourbon, and french fries, she sees every morning as an invitation to daily conversion and starts her day with the question: "How will I serve God today?"

Allison Gingras created the Stay Connected Journals for Catholic Women, including her books *The Gift of Invitation* and *Seeking Peace.* She shares her Catholic faith and her always-evolving relationship with Jesus with wit, a little wisdom, and many examples of how it is lived in the everyday, ordinary of life.

Pat Gohn is the author of *All In* and *Blessed, Beautiful, and Bodacious.* Learn more about her work as a retreat leader, editor, and host of the *Among Women* podcast at PatGohn.net.

Jenna Guizar is a wife and mama in sunny Arizona. She loves spending time with her barber husband, their four daughters, and their son. After falling in love with the Lord through deep, faithful friends who prayed and spoke hope into her life, Jenna established the website Blessed Is She as a mission ground to help other women fall more in love with the Lord and into deeper friendships with one another.

Sherry Hayes-Peirce serves the Lord as a digital disciple across social media. She is the digital engagement director and a lector at her parish, American Martyrs Catholic Community, in Manhattan Beach, California. She writes monthly articles for CatholicMom.com and the *Hawaii Catholic Herald.* Recently widowed, Sherry is grateful to God for her two adorable grandchildren, Cooper and Addison; she always sees her husband, Brad, in them.

Lisa M. Hendey is the founder of CatholicMom.com, and the daughter of her beloved mother, Anne, who always believed in and supported the mission of CatholicMom.com, and who died on April 29, 2021. Anne lifted up and inspired every element of Lisa's life, including her ministry as the bestselling author of works for children and adults, including *I'm a Saint in the Making*, *The Grace of Yes*, and the Chime Travelers series. An international speaker and podcaster, Lisa lives online at www.lisahendey.com and in real life with her husband, Greg, in Los Angeles, California.

Christy Isinger is the mom to five loud children and lives in the northern wilds of Canada. When not homeschooling, she is cohost of the *Fountains of Carrots* podcast, is a contributing writer for Blessed Is She, and writes periodically for various Catholic publications.

Christina Dehan Jaloway is a disciple, wife, and mother of two. She received her BA and MA in theology from the University of Notre Dame. Before getting married in 2016, she taught high school theology (her dream job) for nine years and was a blogger and speaker. She lives with her family in beautiful Austin, Texas.

Emily Jaminet is a wife, mother of seven children, author, radio personality, and executive director of the Sacred Heart Enthronement Network, www. welcomeHisHeart.com. Her most recent book is *Secrets of the Sacred Heart*, published by Ave Maria Press.

Mary Ann Jepsen has been married to her husband, Stephen, since 1984 and is mother of four adult sons and two daughters-in-law. She is a licensed professional clinical counselor and owner of Covenant Integrative Counseling Services in the Columbus, Ohio, metropolitan area. Mary Ann was a Catholic radio host for twelve years and a critical-care registered nurse for ten years.

Kelly Johnson is grateful for her family; she lives with her husband, Bob, and college-aged boys in Downers Grove, Illinois. Kelly is the adult faith formation director at St. Mary of Gostyn Catholic Church, the cofounder of Nourish for Caregivers, and coauthor of *The Caregiver's Companion: A Christ-Centered Journal to Nourish Your Soul*.

Maria Morera Johnson and her husband share a home on Mon Louis Island, Alabama, with Otis, their rescue pup, and Ernest, a very territorial pelican. Maria is the author of several award-winning books published by Ave Maria Press, and enjoys writing and speaking about the Catholic faith.

Deb Kelsey-Davis and her husband, Steve, reside in Lake Barrington, Illinois, with their two furry-faced kids, who keep them company now that their two adult children are off and on their own. Deb is cofounder of Nourish for Caregivers, and spends time on social media nourishing caregivers in both public and private Nourish communities.

When she isn't enjoying the Great Lakes, **Clare Kilbane** lives in South Bend, Indiana, with her husband, daughter, and two Glen of Imaal Terriers. She is a faculty member at the University of Notre Dame and works for the McGrath Institute for Church Life.

Justina Kopp is a stay-at-home mom living in the Twin Cities, Minnesota, with her husband, Matthew, and their quadruplet four-year-olds and energetic bernedoodle puppy. Justina is a 2013 graduate of the University of St. Thomas–Minnesota, where she studied Catholic Studies and Biology, and she currently serves on the university's advisory board of the Center for Catholic Studies.

Marcia Lane-McGee is a writer, speaker, and podcaster who was born and raised in Chicago, Illinois. The oldest of her four sisters and three brothers, she isn't bossy . . . she's just confident in her leadership skills. She puts those skills into action running Mooseheart Child City and School as a family teacher, just forty miles west of her hometown.

Mary Lenaburg is a full-time Catholic speaker and the author of the award-winning *Be Brave in the Scared* and *Be Bold in the Broken*. She and her family make their home in Virginia.

Born and raised in Muslim Turkey, **Derya Little** rejected her family's Islamic faith and became an atheist after her parents' divorce. During her stormy adolescence, she tried to convince a Christian that there is no God but was converted to Christ instead. During her doctoral studies in England, she entered the Catholic Church. Nowadays, she lives in a small town with her husband and four children, enjoying coffee, kissing booboos, and writing about the worlds she imagines. She can be found at deryalittle.com and on social media.

Sarah Mackenzie is the founder and host of *The Read-Aloud Revival*, a podcast and online community that helps parents make meaningful and lasting connections with their kids through books. She is the author of *The Read-Aloud Family* and *Teaching from Rest: A Homeschooler's Guide to Unshakable Peace*, and lives in the Northwest with her husband, Andrew, and their six kids.

Maurisa Mayerle and her husband of more than thirty years, Chris, currently live in beautiful Utah. They are parents to seven and grandparents to two amazing and unique human beings. Maurisa writes regularly at fishersofbrokenmen.com.

Katie Prejean McGrady is an international Catholic speaker, award-winning author, and host of *The Katie McGrady Show* on Sirius XM. She serves as a lay consultant to the USCCB Committee for Youth and Young Adult Ministry, writes a monthly column for the Catholic News Service, and hosts the *Ave Explores* podcast. She lives in Louisiana with her family.

Colleen C. Mitchell is the bestselling author of *Who Does He Say You Are? Women Transformed by Christ in the Gospels* and *When We Were Eve: Uncovering the Woman God Created You to Be*. She resides in Fort Wayne, Indiana, where she is a social worker and mother to five sons. She is an enthusiast of football, Christmas decorations, good wine, dark chocolate, good cries, and belly laughs.

Annabelle Moseley is a poet and author, most recently of *Sacred Braille: The Rosary as Masterpiece* (EnRoute, 2019); a professor of theology; and a Catholic broadcaster with two popular podcasts on WCAT Radio. She also makes regular appearances on Relevant Radio and writes a monthly column for Aleteia. She is grateful for the domestic church she has built with her husband in the North Shore of Long Island, along with their children, who provide a generous daily supply of laughter.

Lauren Nelson is married and the mother of two daughters, Alice and Mia. She has a bachelor of arts in theology and is pursuing her master's in pastoral studies. She works in religious education and lives in Illinois.

Andi Oney is an international Catholic evangelist, wife, and mother from the New Orleans area who is known for her anointed teaching and exhortation. She is the author of *Extravagant Praise: Our History, Heritage, and Hope* and *Mary's Life in the Holy Spirit: A Model for Us*. Andi is a senior team member of Hope and Purpose Ministries.

Susanna Parent is a freelance writer who begins her mornings brewing French press coffee in the home she shares with her husband and daughter in the Twin Cities, Minnesota. When the sun sets, you'll find her with friends enjoying a glass of red wine, preferably outside underneath twinkly lights, or brainstorming her family's next new adventure. To explore tools and resources for your next holy hour, check out her blogpost "How to Make a Holy Hour" on the Blessed Is She website.

Dorothy Pilarski, founder of CatholicMomsGroup.com and DynamicWomenFaith.com, is on a mission to revive the vocation of motherhood. In partnership with the Archdiocese of Toronto, she has created a Catholic Mothers Group Starter Kit and has worked with more than forty parishes internationally in starting mothers' groups.

Sarah A. Reinhard is a wife, mom, and author. When she's not chasing kids, chugging coffee, or juggling work, Sarah is usually trying to stay up to read just one . . . more . . . chapter. She's online at Snoring Scholar, and lives with her family in a beautiful farmhouse near Columbus, Ohio.

Andrea Remke is a widowed mother of four children. Her husband, Matthew, lost a cancer battle in 2017 when her children were ten, seven, seven, and five. She has a degree in mass communications from Saint Mary's College, Notre Dame, Indiana. She is a freelance writer and blogger who lives in Phoenix, Arizona, with her children and a quite human-like German shepherd named Juno.

Bonnie Rodgers and her husband, Dennis Kronenberg, are transplants to the greater Boston area from Western Massachusetts. Their three young-adult children have brought many great adventures into their lives. Bonnie is the producer of CatholicTV's signature talk show, *This Is the Day.*

Leah Libresco Sargeant grew up an atheist, picked a fight with the smartest wrong people she knew, and was received into the Catholic Church in 2012. She is the author of *Arriving at Amen* and *Building the Benedict Option.*

Elizabeth Scalia is a Benedictine Oblate and the author of several books, including the award-winning *Strange Gods* and *Little Sins Mean a Lot.* She is Word on Fire's editor at large and blogs as "The Anchoress." She is married and lives on Long Island.

Lyrissa Sheptak resides in Alberta, Canada, where, when she isn't tending to the ministry of her family of six, she finds time to tap into her creative side. Lyrissa loves to touch people's hearts through the written word, focusing especially on the beauty of Catholicism and evangelization, as well as her Ukrainian culture. She is the managing editor of *Nasha Doroha* magazine.

Speaker and award-winning singer/songwriter **Trisha Short** is best known by Catholics as the producer and one of the singers of "The Chaplet of Divine Mercy in Song" on EWTN. Trish and her husband, Matt, run a multimedia ministry from their home studio in Fort Worth, Texas. They share their busy life with grandchildren Lee and Ivan and one very controlling cat named Pebbles.

Stephanie A. Sibal is the publicity manager at Ave Maria Press. She has two adult sons, a daughter-in-law, and a dog, and is the stepmother of four. She and her husband, Tom, live as almost–empty nesters in Goshen, Indiana, and attend St. Pius X Catholic Church in Granger, where Stephanie is a lector.

Mallory Smyth is a content creator at Walking with Purpose. She is a Catholic speaker and author of the book *Rekindled: How Jesus Brought Me Back to the Catholic Church and Set My Heart on Fire.* She lives in Denver with her husband and four children.

Daria Sockey and her husband, Bill, live in rural northwest Pennsylvania. They are parents of seven adult children. She is also director of faith formation for her parish, St. Joseph in Oil City, Pennsylvania. She is the author of *The Everyday Catholic's Guide to the Liturgy of the Hours* (Franciscan Media) and has written for many Catholic publications.

Elizabeth Sri and her Catholic theologian husband Edward Sri are raising their eight children in sunny Colorado. She blogs at *Born to Do This* and serves on the board of directors for Life-Giving Wounds, a Catholic ministry for adult children of divorce.

Corynne Staresinic is the founder and executive director of The Catholic Woman, a nonprofit illustrating the many faces and vocations of women in the Church to show young Catholic women that they have a place in the Church. She is an editor, photographer, and convert to Catholicism. She lives in Cincinnati with her husband and kids.

Haley Stewart is a Catholic convert, mother of four, and the award-winning author of *The Grace of Enough: Pursuing Less and Living More in a Throwaway Culture*. She is also a speaker, a fellow of the Word on Fire Institute, and cohost of the *Fountains of Carrots* podcast.

Rose Sweet is a Catholic author, retreat leader, conference speaker, pilgrimage leader, and certified life coach specializing in helping others effectively, practically, and joyfully put their religion into all their relationships. She lives in hot, sunny Palm Desert, California, with her husband, Bob.

Barb Szyszkiewicz is a wife, mom of three young adults, and Secular Franciscan. She is an editor at Catholic Mom.com and a music minister at her parish, and enjoys writing, cooking, and reading.

Theresa Thomas and her husband, David, live in the countryside of Indiana, where they raised their nine children, homeschooled for twenty-five years, and aim to live a simple, good life, following God's promptings. A freelance writer, Theresa has been a family columnist at *Today's Catholic News* since 2005 and has contributed to several books in the *Amazing Grace* (Ascension Press) series. She is coauthor of *Stories for the Homeschool Heart* (Bezalel Books, 2010) and *Big Hearted: Inspiring Stories from Everyday Families* (Sophia Press, 2013).

Kendra Tierney lives in an *It's a Wonderful Life*–style fixer-upper in the wilds of unincorporated Los Angeles County with her husband and their ten kids, aged one to eighteen. She shares her passion for obscure Catholic traditions through her blog *Catholic All Year*, social media, and books including *The Catholic All Year Compendium: Liturgical Living for Real Life* and *O Come Emmanuel: Advent Reflections on the Jesse Tree for Families*.

Elizabeth A. Tomlin is the author of *Joyful Momentum: Growing and Sustaining Vibrant Women's Groups* and general counsel to the Archdiocese for the Military Services, USA. Elizabeth, her husband, Greg, their three children, and their naughty chocolate lab puppy are an army family.

Luz Torres is a social media specialist at Holy Cross Family Ministries in North Easton, Massachusetts. The mother of two wonderful daughters and a grandmother, she enjoys creating memories with her family and being out in nature—especially with her grandson, who loves Grandma's cooking!

Stacy A. Trasancos and her husband, José, live in Hideaway, Texas. Together, with the spiritual guidance of Bishop Joseph Strickland, they run Children of God for Life to fight the use of aborted children in scientific research.

Jenny Uebbing and her husband, Dave, live in Denver, Colorado, with their kids and an ever-expanding to-do list of home improvements to combat the effects of living with half a dozen children. In her spare time Jenny manages Off the Charts, an NFP membership site, and authors the popular blog *Mama Needs Coffee*.

Kendra Von Esh is a recovered corporate executive who left it all behind to help others deepen their relationship with God. She is now a speaker, evangelist, author, podcaster, and social media enthusiast. The love of her husband, Jeff, support from her two stepchildren, and many wet kisses from their dogs made it all possible.

Kelly M. Wahlquist is the founder of WINE: Women in the New Evangelization and director of the Archbishop Flynn Catechetical Institute. She is the author of *Created to Relate: God's Design for Peace & Joy*, and the creator and editor of *Walk in Her Sandals: Experiencing Christ's Passion through the Eyes of Women* and *Gaze upon Jesus: Experiencing Christ's Childhood through the Eyes of Women*.

Susan Wallace has one daughter and is now . . . joyfully . . . a grandmother to a rambunctious little boy. She lives in the small town of Plympton, Massachusetts, which boasts more horses (number unknown) than people (2,600). Her hobbies of pottery making and reading provide relaxation from her work as a marketer for Holy Cross Family Ministries, where she is often heard reminding everyone she meets, "The family that prays together stays together" (Ven. Patrick Peyton's famous message).

Katie Warner is a Catholic homeschooling mom, a popular Catholic children's book author (you can peruse titles at FirstFaithTreasury.com), and the writer behind a prayer journal series with titles that include *A Parent Who Prays* and *A Spouse Who Prays*. She writes for the *National Catholic Register* and helps others return to the Church through Catholics Come Home, but expends most of her energy living the introvert life at home, relishing the changing seasons in Georgia with her husband and fellow book-loving children.

Kathryn Whitaker is the author of *Live Big, Love Bigger*, an award-winning book about living an intentional, hell yes, kind of life. She's a Catholic convert and sixth-generation Texan who lives in Austin with her husband and six children. You can find her online at kathrynwhitaker.net and on social media @kathrynwhitakertx.

Kate Wicker is a wife, mom of five, speaker, and author of *Getting Past Perfect: Finding Joy & Grace in the Messiness of Motherhood* (a 2018 Catholic Press Association Award Winner) and *Weightless: Making Peace with Your Body.* To learn more about her writing and life, visit KateWicker.com.

Christy Wilkens has been married to her husband, Todd, since 2002. Over that time they have had six children; eight houses; four parishes; various dogs, cats, and lizards; and many, many arguments and reconciliations. She is the author of *Awakening at Lourdes* and a contributing writer for Catholic Mom. com, Blessed Is She, and Accepting the Gift. She lives near Austin, Texas.

Catholic convert **Jaymie Stuart Wolfe** is a wife and mother of eight grown children living in the Archdiocese of New Orleans. On her site One More Basket, Jaymie provides a wide range of editorial services and offers events that inspire and evangelize through word and song.

Eileen Zimak is a mom of two who is striving to "let go and let God," and will be working on this for the rest of her life. She lives in New Jersey with her husband, Gary, and her twin daughters, Mary and Elizabeth.

Heidi Hess Saxton is an award-winning author and a senior acquisitions editor at Ave Maria Press. She has written or compiled a number of books, including *Advent with Saint Teresa of Calcutta*, which won a second-place award from the Catholic Press Association. She is the editor of *Forgiveness Makes You Free*.

Saxton has appeared on EWTN's *Women of Grace*, *Catholic Connection*, *Kresta in the Afternoon*, *The Drew Mariani Show*, and the *Son Rise Morning Show*. She earned bachelor's degrees from Bethany College of Missions and Azusa Pacific University and a master's degree in theology from Sacred Heart Major Seminary.

She lives in the South Bend, Indiana, area with her family.

Heidihesssaxton.blog
Facebook: A Life on the Road Less Traveled
Twitter: @hsaxton
Instagram: @heidihesssaxton1999
Pinterest: heidihesssaxton

Emily Wilson Hussem is an international speaker, author, and YouTuber who runs a global ministry for women. She is the bestselling and award-winning author of *Go Bravely*, *Awaken My Heart*, and the *Go Bravely Companion Journal*.

AVE
AVE MARIA PRESS

Founded in 1865, Ave Maria Press,
a ministry of the Congregation of
Holy Cross, is a Catholic publishing
company that serves the spiritual and
formative needs of the Church and its
schools, institutions, and ministers;
Christian individuals and families; and
others seeking spiritual nourishment.

For a complete listing of titles from

Ave Maria Press

Sorin Books

Forest of Peace

Christian Classics

visit www.avemariapress.com

AVE MARIA PRESS
Notre Dame, IN
A Ministry of the United States Province of Holy Cross